Individual and Collective Responsibility

MASSACRE AT MY LAI

I think all American citizens must share in Calley's guilt. I wonder how many people in the country last night and people in the State Department and generals in the Army had a good night's sleep.

—Captain Ernest Medina, March 30, 1971

I do not believe that we should hold any one person responsible for My Lai. I do not believe that we should hold any one person or the nation responsible. If you want to hold someone responsible, I think the only one you could point to would be God.

—Wilbur Hamman, Psychiatrist, Defense Witness

Individual and Collective Responsibility

MASSACRE AT MY LAI

Edited by Peter A. French

Illustrations by Jane Sterrett

SCHENKMAN PUBLISHING COMPANY
Cambridge, Massachusetts

ISSUES IN CONTEMPORARY ETHICS

A Schenkman Series Edited by Peter French

USELESS CRIME: The Manson Family
Edited by David E. Cooper

CONSCIENTIOUS ACTIONS:
The Revelation of the
Pentagon Papers
Edited by Peter French

PUNISHMENT: Attica
Edited by Milton Goldinger

UTOPIA/DYSTOPIA?
Edited by Peyton Richter

ASSASSINATION
Edited by Harold Zellner

ABORTION
Edited by Robert L. Perkins

Schenkman Publishing Company
Cambridge, Massachusetts 02138

Library of Congress Catalog Card Number: 72-81522
Printed in the United States of America

CONTENTS

PREFACE

This is the first volume of a new series of books which deal with contemporary ethical issues. Each volume features contributions written specifically for the volume by outstanding moral philosophers. The contributors did not have access to each other's articles but have independently developed their views on the issue There is amazingly little repetition, testifying to the breadth and perhaps also to the importance of the issues. An attempt has of course been made to assure that the contributors represent divergent moral points of view.

First and foremost this is a philosophy series, designed to help us in some comprehensible way with the sometimes overwhelming, always serious, issues of the day. The major example used in this volume, the massacre at My Lai, is to be thought of as the occasion for raising and investigating the moral and legal questions of individual and collective responsibility. We are not trying to pass judgment on Lt. Calley, his company, or his superiors; that has been done and will surely be reviewed. We are not pronouncing a verdict upon the American system; that has also been done, and it will continue to be done in the years of social retrospection which hopefully will follow the Indochina war. Yet neither are we putting off judgment. Instead, the philosophers writing in this volume are examining the grounds for holding various notions of responsibility and the application of such notions to the atrocity that was My Lai. In brief, the aim of this book, and of the series as a whole, is to produce exciting new philosophical contributions to the major ethical controversies of the day.

There are a number of people without whose cooperation this volume would have remained a proposal on the publisher's desk. Obviously, the seven philosophers whose work comprises the body of the book are to be thanked for their outstanding contributions and for their faith in the project from its inception. I am also indebted to Barbara McGinnis for her willingness to aid in locating source material at the library of the University of Minnesota, Morris, to students James Shekleton and Robb Morin for research assistance, to the publisher's managing editor Sheila Segal for guidance and encouragement, and to my wife Sandra for innumerable reasons, including the typing of the manuscript. Many thanks also to Jane Sterrett for her sensitive visual statement on the serious event and philosophical issue. Perhaps I should also acknowledge a debt to Ron Ridenhour, Seymour Hersh, Aubrey Daniel and those others who forced us to face ourselves and our responsibilities, both collective and individual. Surely without their uncommon bravery in revealing to us the problem, the issues of individual and collective responsibility might not be the haunting questions they are to so many Americans and to those who seek to understand Americans.

PETER A. FRENCH

The Responsibility of Monsters and Their Makers

I'm sorry about it: sometimes, my attorneys did to Medina what the prosecutor would do to me. "Now wasn't the real villain in My Lai Captain Medina? And not the poor sweet lieutenant?" But the lieutenant wasn't all so sweet, and the captain was no more a villain than any American from the President down. The guilt: as Medina said, we all as American citizens share it. I agree. . . . I say if there's guilt, we must suffer it.

—"The Concluding Confessions of Lieutenant Calley" by First Lieutenant William L. Calley, Jr. interviewed by John Sack, *Esquire*, Sept. 1971.

I came to realize that the Army's nothing but a Frankenstein monster, and I was a little part of it. America tried to build sort of a superman: a war machine (it may sound ridiculous) that was a peace machine. . . . But remember the story of Dr. Frankenstein? What a good doctor he was at first? How he would build a superman with the smartest brain and the strongest body? . . . But it became uncontrollable. And it just killed. Do not blame the Frankenstein monster, though. The people of the United States did create the United States Army.

—"The Continuing Confessions of Lieutenant Calley," *Esquire*, Feb. 1971.

Lieutenant Calley is not a scapegoat. He is an accomplice.

—(signed) Arthur Barlas. Letter to the editor, *Newsweek*, Mar. 3, 1971.

THREE RATHER PUZZLING COMMENTS, two made by Lt. Calley, are indicative of the complex issues we confront. On the surface, the two remarks of Lt. Calley suggest that guilt and blame for the massacre at My Lai should not be ascribed to the individual executors of the act, but instead to a collective which, we may assume, was not even aware of the massacre being perpetrated. Lt. Calley seems to differentiate between guilt and blame, and we should not confuse them as we analyze his statements. The first claim, call it "the first ascription," is concerned with guilt, specifically, guilt shared by members of a collective of "all as American citizens." The second ascription speaks of blame. Again blame is placed on a collective of "the people of the United States." The first ascription includes Lt. Calley and the soldiers under his command within the group sharing guilt; the second is not quite so clear as to the composition of the group, and, in fact, if Calley's analogy between the Army and the Frankenstein monster is borne out, would seem to absolve the soldiers of blame. The apparent confusion here on Calley's part concerning just who is guilty and who is deserving of blame indicates the complexity of the philosophical issues of responsibility raised by the My Lai massacre.

"Guilt" has been traced back to the notion of debt. The Latin *debitum* in the Lord's Prayer and in Matthew XVIII 27 is translated in Old English as *gylt*. The substantive sense of *gylt* as debt has often been inferred to be the primary sense of the term, which may explain certain common expressions such as "the guilty must pay" and "paying one's debt to society." But clearly this is not the only ordinary use of "guilt." A debt can be transferred; guilt cannot. The family of the deceased may be bound to pay his outstanding debts but not to assume the guilt for his trespasses of law. The substantive sense of "guilt' is seldom really in common use. "The guilt lies here," we may say, or "Pin the guilt on him," but, as with many other evaluative words, we are more inclined to use the adjectival sense: "He is the guilty one," "The guilty party will be discovered." There is, however, a substantive sense of "the state of guilt" as the state of having committed an act which merits condemnation and reproach. This distinction normally refers to a legal state, such as bankruptcy, with no specific characteristics other than the fact that the individual in question has been found guilty. Even then the inclination is to avoid the substantive definition of that state and say simply, "He is guilty." To the question, "What state is he in?" one might respond, "anguish, delirium, agitation, shock,"—but "guilt"? What is it like to be in a state of guilt?

Perhaps what is normally meant is that one recognizes that he could be shown to be delinquent, that one knows or can be persuaded that he has been at fault, that one accepts culpability. But there is a marked difference between this kind of legal assessment of the "state of guilt" and what we normally mean when we say something like, "He is in a state of shock." In brief, being in a state of guilt is to be "guilty of," which does not entail "being convicted of. . . ." It is not to have a characteristic set of facial expressions, mental processes, dispositions, or whatever. To be in a "state of guilt" means to be "guilty of . . . ," which does not necessarily entail "being convicted of . . . ." To be "guilty of . . ." is to have been in transgression of the law (moral or legal) and not able to support any one of a number of specific pleas, i.e. accident, duress, insanity (though one may be "guilty but insane" in legal parlance). In this regard careful attention should be paid to Kurt Baier's analysis of the notion of guilt and the relationship between it and various forms of responsibility.

There are surely many ways in which members of collectives may be said to share the guilt for an act or even to be equally guilty of the same act. If a bank robbery planned and executed by three persons is foiled and all three captured, they will all, there being no demonstrable conditions of the sort that one of them was acting under duress (fear of his life, etc.), be found guilty of the deed, though they may not be equally responsible for it. By saying that they are collectively guilty we are saying just that the three of them did, in fact, collectively attempt the robbery. In this sense there is no legal question of one being more or less guilty than the others. It might be shown that one of the three bankrobbers possessed certain abilities that were necessary for the crime and that without him the other two would have been unable to carry out the plan. Yet the law does not single out one, the safe cracker, as "more guilty" than the machine gunner who stood guard. If this were a second or third offense for one and not the others, of course he might be liable to greater punishment, but that is not a question of greater guilt.

In cases of collective guilt we usually assume that the members of the collective must actually have committed the criminal or reprehensible act or have contributed in some material way, whether as perpetrators, inciters, abetors, etc., to the commission of the deed. A rather large group of people might be collectively guilty of a crime owing to their various offices in regard to its perpetration. Imagine a large criminal syndicate undertaking. No doubt we would have difficulty determining the extent of each member's contribution, especially when questions of the voluntary nature of each member's participation are raised. What is important here is that if collective responsibility is formulated in terms of guilt then it should amount to but the sum of all individual responsibilities (liabilities). We have not any guarantee, however, that when we are talking of guilt we are also talking of responsibility; for example, there may be cases of a collective's guilt for which only one person is responsible. But it seems reasonable to assume that where guilt is collective those judged guilty must have in some way actually affected the perpetration of the wrong doing. Some, of course, may do so only by refraining from doing what might have altered the circumstances (especially if we are talking of moral guilt). It would seem, however, that all held collectively guilty must have (intentionally?) violated the law (legal or moral).

In regard to the My Lai massacre most of the grounds for the ascription of collective guilt to all of the American people are missing. It might be argued that all Americans who contribute taxes to the government without protest place themselves voluntarily in the position of inciters. This may be true in the case of the Vietnam war taken as a whole or even of the bombing raids on the North Vietnamese, but it is doubtful that it can be made to apply in the case of the massacre. In the first place, the massacre, at least according to officialdom, was an aberration; it was not government policy nor, for that matter, an act of the war as such. The payment of taxes did not "incite" it. In what sense can we all be guilty without having violated any law, without having performed any specific voluntary act in regard to the massacre? It might be suggested that the hierarchical system of the armed forces and the whole idea that the armies of a country represent the people of that country make superiors guilty for the behavior of those under their command and all of us guilty for the actions of those in the field. But this may be to confuse "being guilty" with "having a vicarious liability" (being worthy of blame). There is a long history of examples of the notion of vicarious individual and collective liability in both legal and moral matters. Stanley Bates discusses some of these. The questions of vicarious individual and collective liability often arise in such business institutions as suretyship and agency, but these situations do not really help us to understand Calley's claim that all Americans are collectively guilty of the My Lai massacre. In the case of agency, the misconduct of an agent makes his employer liable for restitution, etc. but the fault or guilt for the deed in question does not transfer also to the employer. The employer, if his agent were discovered to have injured a patron, may be held liable to compensate the injured party, but he cannot be criminally prosecuted for the wrong doing unless he ordered his agent to commit the criminal act or, if after learning of the deed, he demonstrated his assent to its performance by his agent. Fault and guilt cannot be borne vicariously. Thus, if all Americans are guilty of the massacre at My Lai, it must be shown that they all in some way contributed materially to the monstrous acts performed that day in March 1968.

There is nevertheless a somewhat common sense of collective guilt which allows ascription to a relatively random group when some common feature of the group's character is productive of the harm. Consider the following comment about ghetto schools from Jonathon Kozol's *Death at an Early Age*:

> All white people . . . are implicated . . . so long as we participate in America in a normal way and attempt to go on leading normal lives while any race is being cheated and tormented.

It has been argued that due to the assent of the majority of white Americans to policy which reflects their common attitudes, customs, mores, even religious biases, minorities are caused to suffer and often die. Stanley Bates maintains that it is a myth that individuals can exist apart from and prior to social structure and that we are often implicated even in those social acts which we would not freely have chosen. If certain white Americans are exempt from guilt for the plight of non-white minorities, what would count as grounds for their exclusion? Virginia Held and Haskell Fain deal in different ways with this sort of problem.

H. D. Lewis takes the view that guilt appears to be collective only in sum of the individual guilt of the members. Thus he suggests that "collective responsibility" is but a "sum term" and that there is no sense of collective responsibility where individuals cannot be specifically cited. David Cooper and Virginia Held dispute the applicability of such a view (which in some forms is called methodological individualism). R. S. Downie, on the other hand, offers reasons for holding an individualist position by reference to the idea of social role acceptance. Perhaps, though, there is an underlying confusion in the tendency to treat "guilt" and "responsibility" as interchangeable, making it unclear how we might distinguish members of the collective as "guilty but not responsible, guilty but of diminished responsibility, responsible but not really guilty."

The second ascription of Lt. Calley, the one which draws the analogy between the Army and the Frankenstein monster, suggests grounds other than guilt for the ascription of responsibility to the collective. We are told not to blame the monster for its actions. The blame lies with the maker even, it would appear, if the maker is no longer in control or not aware of the doings of the monster. Dr. Frankenstein himself says:

> I am the assassin of those most innocent victims; they died by my machinations. A thousand times would I have shed my own blood, drop by drop, to have saved their lives; but I could not.
>
> —*Frankenstein* by Mary Shelley

We should guard, however, against the reduction of this idea to the untenable position that parents are guilty of the crimes their offspring commit. Certain societal benefits might be derived should the practice be adopted of punishing parents for the delinquent behavior of their children, but that is not necessarily to say that the parents would be guilty of their children's crimes. The point is that one can be blameworthy, perhaps even punishable in regard to some offenses, though he is not guilty, which raises again the issue as already suggested of whether liability can be clearly separated from the question of guilt.

Blameworthiness often has been analytically tied to fault or guilt, but there are other senses of being "to blame" than that of having perpetrated the specific ill deed. Notice these different uses of "blame":

1. The whole football team's to blame for the loss to Podunk State.
2. Blame the war on the past administration.
3. There's no doubt that he stole the car, but I blame the parents.
4. In our town very few people stopped at that stop sign at the deserted intersection. Recently, however, there was a multiple car accident at that place which claimed the lives of four children. Even though only one citizen of our town caused the disaster, we all share the blame.

In the first example a collective is blamed, but there may be a reluctance to single out any individual member of the football team. It's not that any one of the team members was at fault; they simply lacked something in their overall play. The third example is similar to those of suretyship and agency: the parents are not guilty of car theft, or of anything specifically criminal, just as Dr. Frankenstein, who was physically incapable of those acts of violence, was not guilty of the monster's suitably monstrous crimes.

Although the noun form of "blame" is often taken to be a synonym for "guilt" and "fault," it has already been shown that this is not always the case. Where an offense has occurred the senses of responsibility to be ascribed often can be delineated by the choice of words from among these terms: x is at fault, y bears the guilt, z deserves the blame. Surely in the majority of cases x, y, and z will all be the same person, but in other important cases they may be distinct individuals or collectives.

"Fault," used as a noun, generally applies to the cause of some failure, as in "It was Johnny's fault; he fumbled on the ten yard line." Fault does not entail intention. "Guilt," however, is generally applied (though there are exceptional cases) in cases of willful breaches of a code of conduct, legal or moral. "Blame," on the other hand, stresses the censure that is coincidental with one's being held liable for some sub-standard behavior or trait of character. What counts as sufficient grounds for the ascription of blame? First let us eliminate all those grounds on which unacceptable excuses from blame are based. If not having intended the act, as in Frankenstein's case, is not always an excuse which frees one from the responsibility, then intention, perhaps even voluntariness, cannot be analytically tied to liability. Dr. Frankenstein is liable (at least morally so) for the specific acts of his monster, regardless of Dr. Frankenstein's intent. His plea to the effect that it (his monster) had gotten out of control (his control) is unacceptable. Referring to the fourth example above, we are to blame, again morally; we all run the stop sign, and, though none of us ever does so with intent to cause accidents, any one of us could have done so on that one tragic occasion; after all, we did it all the time. The point might be that one is to blame if he should have known in advance what dire consequences might likely occur and should thereby have acted otherwise than he did, whether or not he intended the actual outcome.

Another unacceptable excuse from blame is the plea of physical incapability. The plea of ignorance, to which Aristotle lent importance, seems also to be wanting. Dr. Frankenstein's knowledge or lack of it in regard to the acts of his monster does not relieve him of all blame. Imagine situations in which it might be said, "I don't care whether you knew it was going on or not, you're responsible." The famous war crimes trial of General Yamashita would be a prime example. In this regard attention should be paid to Stanley Bates' article where he maintains that vicarious liability must be based on some actual liability, as in the case where Yamashita is actually liable for the breakdown of troop discipline and thereby vicariously liable for the war crimes of his troops. Might not the same be said in an analogous way of Dr. Frankenstein and his monster and of the "people of the United States" and Charlie Company?

It has already been mentioned that "blame" is appropriately used to place censure on those whose behavior is held to be sub-standard. Parents are to blame for their children's delinquency when their parenthood has not been up to the quality generally expected in the community. The football team is to blame for its loss to Podunk because the character of its team effort fell below par. When we place the blame on the past administration we cite it for performance below that expected of officials. Individuals and collectives, then, are said to be responsible and blameworthy when their performances or character fail to reach a certain standard. But what determines the standard and what determines who belongs to the collective?

Lt. Calley's second ascription of collective responsibility could perhaps be understood as the claim that Americans as a group failed to perform as they could have been expected. By our lack of preventive action, by our willingness to allow ourselves to be governed poorly, or by our failure to grasp the significance of what we were doing, we showed ourselves to be sub-standard, that is either below that standard that we set for ourselves traditionally or below the standard expected of the people of all nations in regard to international behavior. We should have known better, Calley suggests. We are thereby blameworthy and, if the Frankenstein analogy is appropriate, then we bear the blame for that specific atrocity which was My Lai. All Americans thereby might be collectively vicariously liable for the My Lai massacre. But even at that one wants to make significant exceptions.

Clearly the concept of collective responsibility is not without difficulties, and the weight of those difficulties may be such to persuade us that it is not a helpful moral notion, that it may have only practical legal uses. We may, in fact, be persuaded that there is no viable moral notion of collective responsibility. H. D. Lewis defends the position that moral responsibility can be ascribed only to individuals. This would assume that every ascription of collective responsibility either reduces to the claim that each member of the group is individually responsible or that the very notion of collective responsibility evades moral descriptions of responsibility. The strength of Lewis's view is, no doubt, that it eliminates the difficult position of defending a view in which someone can be held responsible for the acts of another.

Can the responsibility of a group be more than the sum of the responsibilities of its members? Certain of our examples would suggest that a reduction of collective responsibility to specific individual responsibilities is not always appropriate, but perhaps the notion of responsibility in those cases is confused. R. S. Downie and Kurt Baier attempt to clarify some of these issues, and Baier gives a detailed account of various senses of responsibility. Yet another problem is that it seems unfair to ascribe collective responsibility to a group which is not clearly structured to receive responsibility. David Cooper suggests that random collections cannot be held collectively responsible. He therefore seeks to identify "the system" which might be held responsible in the My Lai case. Virginia Held, on the other hand, argues that under certain specified conditions a random group can bear responsibility; she argues that Charlie Company can be held responsible for the massacre at My Lai, though it is basically a random collectivity, because reasonable alternatives were open to its members.

There remains, then, the third quotation, the view that Lt. Calley is not a scapegoat but an accomplice. This remark reveals yet another aspect of the responsibility problems involving the massacre case, though it is a legal and not a specifically moral one. An accomplice is someone associated in an endeavor with another, the latter being the principal perpetrator. In the commission of a crime an accomplice is not the principal offender, though often clear distinctions are not drawn when the case is adjudicated, i.e. Angela Davis's trial for murder as an accomplice. If Calley is an accomplice, who is the principal? Certain aspects of this question suggest an examination of the relationship between commands and obligations.

Two cases from the Leipzig war crimes trials which followed the First World War are indicative of the issue. One is the trial of Lieutenant Karl Neumann (see Mullins, *The Leipzig Trials,* 1921). Neumann was a Commander of a German submarine. He admitted the torpedoing of a British hospital ship, *Dover Castle,* but he pleaded that he was only carrying out an order of the German Admiralty. That order, as it appears, was that all enemy hospital ships which had not six weeks previously reported their course and kept to it when leaving Greece would be regarded as vessels of war and were liable to attack. The order was based on the Admiralty's belief that its enemies were utilizing hospital ships for decidedly military purposes. The Admiralty believed that it was acting consistent with international law if such hospital ships were being put to military use. Because the Admiralty was the highest authority over a Commander of a submarine, Lt. Neumann was therefore duty bound to obey the order, and in this service matter, his plea continued, the *Dover Castle* was in violation of the hospital ship procedure.

The court quoted the German Military Penal Code, section 47, which states that a subordinate who acts in conformity with orders is liable to punishment as an accomplice if he knows the acts ordered of him by his superiors are violations of the civil or military law. Lt. Neumann's act, however, was not of this sort. He was following the orders of his superior which he considered reasonable and binding. The court therefore ruled that he was not to be held responsible for the sinking of the hospital ship.

The other case is that of Lieutenants Ludwig Dithmar and Johann Boldt. Both lieutenants were officers in the submarine U-86, Captain Helmuth Patzig commanding. On the night of June 27, 1918, they (Patzig with Dithmar and Boldt) torpedoed the British hospital ship *Llandovery Castle* and subsequently fired on the lifeboats which contained the crew of the sunken ship. The two lieutenants had taken part in the torpedoing of the hospital ship under the orders of the captain. The three officers, however, had conferred after the *Llandovery Castle* had sunk and agreed to destroy all witnesses by sinking the lifeboats which contained 234 survivors.

The court ruled that the lieutenants were not guilty of the torpedoing of the hospital ship, in effect accepting the plea of superior orders, even though the act was a clear violation of international law. The court held, however, that defendants Dithmar and Boldt were guilty of aiding and abetting manslaughter in firing upon the lifeboats. (The captain was never tried because he couldn't be found.) The court maintained:

> Military subordinates are under no obligation to question the order of their superior officer, and they can count upon its legality. But no such confidence can be held to exist, if such an order is universally known to everybody, including also the accused, to be without any doubt whatever against the law. This happens only in rare and exceptional cases. But this case was precisely one of them, for in the present instance, it was perfectly clear to the accused that killing defenseless people in the lifeboats could be nothing else but a breach of the law.

The plea of superior orders was expressly ruled out of the Nuremberg trials, though the defense of one of the accused, Jodl, was built almost solely on that plea. Lt. Calley's lawyers also sought to establish superior orders issued by Captain Ernest Medina as a justification of the lieutenant's behavior at My Lai. Accounts of the court-martial reveal that the defense attempted to show that Calley had been commanded to destroy the village of My Lai 4 and all of its inhabitants and that therefore he had good reason to feel threatened with serious punishment (insubordination as a court-martial offense) should he refuse to obey. When asked the direct examination question, "Why did you give Meadlo the order that if you couldn't get rid of them to waste them?" Calley is reported to have answered, "Because that was my order, sir. That was the order of the day, sir." And to the cross-examination question, "Now at any time did you stop and consider the legality or illegality of those orders?" Calley responded, "No, sir." Calley therefore, it was argued, was compelled to perform the acts he did at My Lai 4. Some have interpreted Calley's feeling of compulsion to obey orders as a justification for his behavior. Some have argued that feeling so compelled, Calley even had an obligation to "waste My Lai."

If Calley had an obligation to destroy My Lai, then clearly he was justified in doing so and would not have been justified had he not destroyed My Lai. In fact, if Calley had such an obligation no amount of justifications for refusal to do so would be acceptable, legally or morally. But even in the context of the Army hierarchy, as the court-martial and the Nuremberg charter show, commands do not obligate unless they are legal. The fact that he may have been commanded (though the command was illegal) to waste the village may have been a reason for Calley so doing, but it is not grounds to establish that he would not have been justified in refusing to do so. Perhaps this indicates that Calley has an excuse for "wasting the village," but the acceptability of such an excuse was clearly denied by the court-martial. Kurt Baier provides an analysis of the command/guilt problem in this case, and Haskell Fain discusses the problems that arise when illegality and duty conflict, problems which often occur because of a confusion of morality with legality.

Fain also argues that if Calley's orders were legal then the United States is responsible, and David Cooper examines the grounds for ascription of principal responsibility to the U. S. Army system. If the system can be shown to bear primary responsibility for the atrocities committed then one might accept the view that Calley was an accomplice, not unlike the German lieutenants. Though here we are clearly talking of legal responsibility, there does not seem to be so clear a distinction between principal and accomplice in moral matters, for it is uncertain what, morally speaking, an accomplice would be. This may suggest grounds, then, for understanding the notion of collective responsibility that does not reduce to individual responsibilities as, strictly speaking, a moral notion, contrary to H. D. Lewis's views. The example of the stop sign accident in this regard should warrant thereby close attention.

Returning to the analogy with monsters and their makers, it should be evident that an accomplice bears blame in a way different from that which might be ascribed to a monster. One could say, "The monster was to blame for the young girl's death," much as the fog might be to blame for the collision of two ships. "Blame" here would mean "cause" or "one of the causes" and not blameworthiness of the sort occasioned by sub-standard behavior. Unlike a monster, any accomplice is to blame because he should have known that what he was doing was likely to result in disastrous consequences. The accomplice's behavior may well be described as sub-standard, but by definition a monster's behavior cannot properly so be described. These are, however, only suggestions for dealing with the vast and uncharted region of individual and collective responsibility and its application to the My Lai case. It is left to the contributors to this volume to map in more detail the complexities which underlie such simple sounding expressions as those uttered by Lt. Calley, Mr. Barlas, and the many others who in recent months have found themselves attempting to account for the monstrous human acts that took place in My Lai, March 16, 1968.

HASKELL FAIN

Some Moral Infirmities of Justice

ONE SHOULD BE SUSPICIOUS of philosophical efforts to lighten the individual responsibilities of those who took part in the massacre at My Lai, of attempts to measure what was done at My Lai by anything but the narrowest of legal yardsticks. Particularly so, when *ad hoc* philosophizing is conducted by defense lawyers or by self-serving politicians who are naturally eager to dissolve individual guilt into the murky waters of some vague collective. One should remember that few who approved of the Nuremberg trials were ready to defend those Germans who, locked in a vast machine over which they had no control, by their compliance made possible spectacular crimes. I can recall only one American writer of the period, Dwight MacDonald in *Politics,*[1] who considered the nature and problem of collective responsibility from a German point of view. In those days the concept of collective responsibility was a tool of the prosecution and not of the defense, a means to tar as many Germans as possible with the Nazi brush.

[1] Reprinted in Dwight MacDonald's *Memoirs of a Revolutionist* (New York: Farrar, Straus and Cudahy, 1957), pp. 33–72.

It was the accused, or their defenders, who tried to undermine the notion of collective responsibility.

Discussion positions are now reversed. The concept of collective responsibility is invoked in behalf of the accused at My Lai, and the prosecution seeks to set applicability limits. Such turnabouts ought to make one skeptical about the concept of collective responsibility itself. Is the idea of collective responsibility a mere rhetorical device, useful for expanding or contracting individual responsibility to suit the occasion? I shall try to defend the integrity of at least one concept of collective responsibility, and indicate how it both resembles and differs from individual responsibility. The main difficulty with various notions of collective responsibility (and there are more than one) is that they seem to have no relevance to judicial procedure, or at least no relevance to that procedure developed in Anglo-American law. One cannot bring to justice persons who were ready and willing to do the very crime which fell to others to carry out. One cannot argue in a court of law that when a crime is committed by many it is judicially wrong to punish a few and allow the rest to go free. I have called this essay "Some Moral Infirmities of Justice" in order to underscore the frustration of attempting to articulate moral intuitions about collective responsibility within legal systems of criminal justice designed to deal with responsibility solely on an individual basis.

GUILT FOR COLLECTIVE ACTIONS

Of all those directly participating in the My Lai massacre, First Lieutenant William Laws Calley, Jr., alone was found by a court to be guilty. The Army did at one time or another charge twenty-five officers and enlisted men for actions in connection with My Lai; only six of these men were actually tried, and the charges against the other nineteen were dismissed. All of the six were acquitted, except for Calley, who was convicted of murder. Those actually charged were only a small fraction of the men who, by the Army's own reckoning, might have had something to do with the incident. 'C' Company, in which Calley commanded the 1st platoon, contained 105 men, and *it* was only one of three infantry companies which had a direct role in the My Lai operation. In addition to infantry, there was "suppressive" fire support by artillery and helicopter gun ship. Beyond that, there were officers in charge of the whole My Lai operation to which a special task force—"Task Force Barker"—had been assigned. This is only the beginning of the search for participants, and why stop there? One of the main difficulties with collective responsibility is that it is a greedy concept, and to preserve its integrity, it is necessary to impose firm limits upon its applicability. Not every American is a murderer, though America's present policies made My Lai possible. Not every American belongs to a collective, all members of which are responsible for murder.

If one of the tasks in developing a valid notion of collective responsibility is to prevent it from becoming too global, another is to distinguish it from individual responsibility. No gain accrues from introducing a notion of collective responsibility which can be analytically dissolved into individual responsibility, plain and simple. Suppose Joe, Willy, Sam, and Tom are members of a gang, and one day they seize a girl and rape her seriatim. We may, if we like, speak here about "*the collective* responsible for the rape" and think of the responsibility of individual members of the gang as somehow derivative from a collective responsibility overshadowing the entire episode. But to what purpose? There was no "collective" rape, though the girl was raped by Joe, Willy, Sam and Tom, *collectively*. True, one can refer to the incident by using the definite singular—*the* rape rather than "the rapes." Still, it would be overstraining grammatical intuition to suppose that very much could be made of this point. *The* rape is nothing but the sum of four separate rapes; each participant is individually responsible for rape, and that responsibility would have been exactly the same had he been the sole miscreant. At most one may hypothesize that membership in the gang enabled some participants to do what they, as individuals, would have been incapable of doing. This, by itself, does not provide a basis for introducing a concept of collective responsibility that can withstand analytical dismemberment.

What is missing in the above example, it may be held, is the idea of *contribution*. If a group of persons participates in some activity, that is not yet sufficient for labeling the activity *collective action,* or for denominating the group as the collective responsible. Individual participation transforms itself into collective action, it may be held, when the entire production is a function of each and every contribution each individual member makes to the whole project. Thus, suppose that it takes four men to move a particular wagon. Can we not bring to bear a concept of "the collective responsible for moving the wagon," and assign responsibility to each member of any quartet who cooperate in moving it? Unlike the rape case, no single individual *could* here be responsible, for, by hypothesis, no person is strong enough to move the wagon without the aid of three other people. This feature does not seem to change the intrinsic nature of each person's individual responsibility, however, for each person is *equally* responsible for moving the wagon. If moving large wagons were a crime, one man with the strength of four who could move a wagon by himself would not be four times as guilty as the normal person in a wagon-moving collective of four. To put the point another way, it seems extrinsic to the nature of certain crimes that it takes more than one person to accomplish them. Why, then, view individual responsibilities differently for crimes requiring collective action than for crimes requiring only lone criminals?

Anglo-American common law is in accord with one's intuitions on this point. Criminal complicity extends to those who plan a crime as well as to those who carry it out; to those who furnish the means beforehand as well as to those who provide protection afterwards. In fact, persons are often found guilty of crimes they could not have perpetrated by themselves. Once again, it seems, the concept of collective responsibility is analytically reducible to that of individual responsibility. If anything was "collectively" interesting about the crime committed at My Lai, it wasn't simply that massacres require the cooperation of many people, including at times the victims. If any concept of collective responsibility can serve to enlarge our understanding of what happened at My Lai, it must involve a collective body not necessarily identical with the class of persons who, directly or indirectly, participated in the massacre.

The Transformation of Individual Responsibility

How can acting in concert change the nature of a crime or the manner in which one views criminal complicity? Perhaps this is the wrong question to ask, for it presupposes that the deeds in which one is interested are necessarily crimes. "The soldier who kills a man in obedience to authority is not guilty of murder," according to Gratian, a twelfth century authority on canon law. And though one may contend, *contra* Gratian, that soldiers who kill while acting under orders can nonetheless be guilty of murder —which was the prosecution's contention in Calley's trial—almost everyone recognizes that various collective frameworks can transform the nature of the individual actions of collective members. Surely it is immoral for one individual to kill another who is innocent of all wrong-doing. Yet when two states are at war, the soldiers of one are enjoined to kill soldiers of the other. It is not correct to say that soldiers of belligerent nations are to be *excused* for killing each other, as one excuses a hunter for accidentally shooting his companion. Nor is it proper to describe the act of a soldier killing an enemy soldier in armed combat as *justifiable* homicide, as one perhaps describes the act of a policeman who shoots a robbery suspect for failure to halt. The word "homicide" means, literally, the act of one human being killing another; and though war itself may appear, abstractly, as the union of many separate "homicidal" acts, the collective nature of the activity seems to change the very substance of the separate acts of which it is composed. It is as improper to label "homicide" the act of a soldier killing an enemy soldier in armed combat, as it is to call "homicide" what the executioner does to the lawfully condemned criminal.

The means by which collectives transform the nature of the acts of their members is a subject of great interest and a perplexing problem in political philosophy. Hobbes, for example, thought that collective activity underwent the necessary conceptual metamorphosis when *commonwealths* were established. A commonwealth, according to Hobbes, is a collective whose members have authorized a sovereign to act in their name. It is the fundamental and mysterious act of authorization that transforms robbery into taxation, homicide into execution, killing into warfare.

One need not accept Hobbes' account to recognize that certain kinds of collectives change the conceptual framework by means of which the acts of individual members are understood, evaluated, or judged. It would be grossly unjust to charge the dutiful public hangman with murder, for the hangman represents the whole collective. If there *could* be a charge of murder, it would have to be directed against the entire collective, the state itself, and not against the individual hangman who is only the agent of the state.

In the armed forces, doing one's duty consists largely in following orders. Were not the members of Company C at My Lai only doing their duty?

> Members of the accused's platoon . . . entered the village . . . and found old men, women, and children, none of them armed, in hootches. Some were eating breakfast. The men in Calley's platoon started gathering them up, some as a result of their training, and others at Calley's orders . . . Calley called to Meadlo and Conti to take care of these people, these women, children, babies, and a few old men. They didn't know what he meant by take care of these people at that time. They didn't know that he had formed his intent to kill them . . . Lieutenant Calley returned and he said to Meadlo and Conti, "Why haven't you taken care of these people?" "We have," Meadlo told him. "We're guarding them." "I mean kill them . . . waste 'em." . . . Calley and Meadlo shot these people, these unarmed and unresisting old men, women, and children. Some people tried to run. They were shot down in cold blood on that trail. Meadlo was crying. It was so repulsive . . . what he had to do at the direction of Lieutenant Calley[2]
>
> —Captain Aubrey M. Daniel, III, Chief Prosecutor

In Calley's trial the prosecution spent no little effort in attempting to prove that Calley was acting on his own authority at My Lai, that no orders given by any superior officer could possibly be interpreted as a command to destroy My Lai and all its inhabitants. This claim was maintained, despite the fact that the My Lai operation was one of numerous so-called "search and destroy" missions in areas suspected of being Viet Cong strongholds. Nor was the devastation of My Lai solely the result of the ravages of Calley's platoon. The 2nd platoon of Company C, led by Lieutenant Stephen Brooks (later killed in Vietnam), also shot down unarmed and unresisting old men, women, and children. The prosecution contended that even if an order "to waste" My Lai had been given Calley by some superior officer, such order would,

[2] Richard Hammer, *The Court-Martial of Lt. Calley* (New York: Coward, McCann & Geoghegan, Inc., 1971), pp. 76–78.

by definition, have been "illegal." That was the most sensitive part of the Government's charge: obedience to orders does not constitute doing one's duty, if the orders themselves are illegal. Determining when a particular military order is legal, however, can be an exceedingly complicated and technical question; it is not the case that any plainly inhumane and immoral order is illegal, as the Government in Calley's trial suggested. The "supreme law of the land," that which provides the test of legality in U. S. courts, is not morality. Nor is it international law. According to the standard interpretation of Article VI of the Constitution, the supreme law of the land is defined by the United States Constitution, U. S. statutes and treaties.

Even if the orders Calley issued *were* illegal, what bearing would that really have had in defining the duties of enlisted men who served under Calley's command? An enlisted man, upon entering service, swears "to obey the orders of the President of the United States and orders of the officers appointed over me, according to regulations and the Uniform Code of Military Justice." (An officer, on the other hand, swears to "well and faithfully discharge the duties of the office upon which I am about to enter." The officer oath contains no explicit reference to obedience. It is perhaps for this reason that no jury in a U. S. Army court-martial can be expected to convict an enlisted man "guilty" of following orders, provided, of course, that the enlisted man is a member of the same Army. After World War II about 1600 war crime defendants were tried by U. S. Army Courts in Germany alone, and over 250 death sentences were carried out, some of them against German enlisted men who followed German orders.) Yet were not the enlisted men who followed Calley's orders at My Lai murderers nonetheless, regardless of the fact that no Army court will convict them? What does the defense "I only followed orders" really amount to?

Many Americans have unpleasant associations with the "follow orders" doctrine, thinking of it, perhaps, as a justification only a Nazi could employ. *Ein Befehl ist ein Befehl* (an order is an order), the automaton barks, and six million pop off to the gas chamber. Nonetheless, in any military organization, one fulfills one's military obligations by obeying orders. Suppose those orders are immoral, or, what is apparently worse, *illegal.* Yet isn't every

American school child taught to obey the law first, question afterwards? Should a law turn out to be unconstitutional, one is enjoined to obey it until its unconstitutionality has been clearly decided by the courts. Do any civics teachers advocate disobedience of laws being tested in the courts, on grounds that there is a serious presumption of those laws being unconstitutional—that is, *illegal*—to begin with? In the armed forces, orders constitute the law of the land. Should the President of the United States order a nuclear attack against another state, those who receive the orders are obliged to carry them out, no matter how insane they may appear. Has Congress declared war? The President has emergency powers, however, and who knows that the United States is not responding to a secret attack already launched? Are orders "to waste" an entire people plainly illegal because they are obviously monstrous? At the Nuremberg trials, a number of German officials were convicted for committing what were called "crimes against peace." The Nuremberg tribunal maintained that aggressive war was forbidden under international law and that, accordingly, orders by heads of states to engage in aggressive war are illegal. But no state ever claimed to be waging *aggressive* war. Hitler maintained that Germany had been attacked by Poland. The United States has accused North Vietnam of aggression. That the United States is waging an aggressive war in South East Asia may be apparent to some, but not to all. Though there can be no doubt that orders "to waste" an entire people are beyond the moral pale, such orders may be legal if they are in response to "aggression." To the extent that the U. S. Constitution, its statutes and treaties are in accord with moral principle, there will be no conflict between conscience and duty. But when there are conflicts, one's prima facie civic duty is to ignore one's conscience.

All this is doubtless commonplace. Yet many Americans really do think that fundamental conflicts between conscience and duty cannot arise in America. Who could read the U. S. Constitution, particularly the Bill of Rights, and not think that, in the last analysis, moral principle must find embodiment in the laws of *this* land; who could not think that the courts, in the end, will always find a way of interpreting the Constitution to bring about the desired concordance? And that, perhaps, is the root of our problem. Having tried so hard from the very beginning to enshrine morality itself in the Constitution—to dot the i's and cross the t's of moral principle—we have not only made our legal framework too awesome but have let the courts become our supreme moral guide. The United States was founded in full awareness of the tyranny of government, and the Constitution, in particular the Bill of Rights, was framed in order to mitigate that tyranny. It is ironic that the ultimate effect of these efforts seems to be a kind of tyranny more dangerous than any that has gone before. The initial, but only partial, coincidence of morality with the law of the land is gradually leading to the usurpation of the former by the latter. The Law of the Land is invoked with the same reverent tone reserved for holy things. It is the American State (not Hegel's Prussia) which has inadvertently become "the Divine Idea as it exists on earth." And if, in defense of that Divine Idea, an order to waste all of North Vietnam can be legal, is an order to waste My Lai so obviously illegal?

In sum: Certain kinds of collectives, such as states, can transform the nature of the individual actions of collective members by legalizing them. Soldiers at war are agents of the state and when they kill they are no more guilty of a crime than public hangmen, provided that their actions are legal. In the overwhelming majority of instances, it is legal to obey the orders of one's superiors, no matter how "repulsive" such orders may appear, no matter how shocking to moral sensibility. If Lt. Calley's orders at My Lai violated some of the warfare rules to which the United States had subscribed and were on that account illegal, that was not something necessarily obvious to the men under Calley's command. What *was* perfectly obvious was that Calley (and others) ordered their men to engage in acts which were morally repulsive; Sergeant Meadlo is reported to have obeyed with tears in his eyes. To suppose that Calley's orders had to have been clearly illegal because they were morally despicable is to make a fundamental error to which Americans, in particular, are prone: to confuse morality with legality. The legality of Calley's orders is a complicated issue; their morality was not. If, for example, one hostile move had been made by any of the Vietnamese civilians at My Lai, that would have changed the entire *legal* setting of the massacre (though not its moral horror). The rules of war under which

Calley was convicted do not apply to combatants not in uniform; there is nothing *illegal* about shooting captured old men, women, and children if they have engaged in illegal acts of warfare, such as setting booby traps without wearing military uniforms. Calley's misfortune, incredible as it seems, was that the prosecution proved that not one act of resistance had been offered by anyone at My Lai.

What light does the concept of legalization throw upon the nature of responsibility? We began by searching for a concept of collective responsibility not reducible to that of individual responsibility. We saw that when an individual participates in a crime as a member of a collective, his responsibility is the same as it would have been were he the sole criminal. Hence, even if the kind of crime perpetrated by the collective were so complicated that it could not have been committed by any single member of the collective alone, this would not change the nature of each criminal's responsibility. We may still hold the collective as a whole to be responsible for the crimes it commits, but criminal responsibility is nonetheless distributed evenly among its members. Nothing new has been added. But when we turn to the obvious cases in which attribution of collective responsibility is not reducible to the responsibility of the members of the collective, we experience a frustration of a different kind. A state may impose the death penalty for violation of any laws, as it pleases, but the executioner is not responsible for murder, any more than is the judge or jury.

Is the United States as a collective responsible for My Lai? That question, instead of being important, turns out to be of little theoretical interest. A slightly different scenario at My Lai, and no one is legally guilty of murder. If the orders issued at My Lai were legal, then the United States is responsible. If they were illegal, then the United States is not responsible. When one is interested in the morality of capital punishment and the responsibility of hangmen, however, it is difficult to find intellectual purchase in a case where the main issue seems to lie in determining whether some hangman exceeded his legal authority. To point the problem: If the collective called "the United States" is responsible for what happened at My Lai, then no member of the collective is responsible for any crime because no crime was committed. State-collectives cannot be guilty of *crime* because when agents of the state, including heads of state, act criminally, their acts are no longer considered to be acts of the collective. On the other hand, if there are persons who are criminally responsible for what happened at My Lai, then the collective called "the United States" is not responsible. Collective responsibility and individual responsibility seem to mutually exclude each other —not a very satisfying state of affairs.

The Responsibility of Those Who Would Serve

Is there a concept of collective responsibility which can enlarge our understanding of what happened at My Lai, one which, moreover, neither makes us lose sight of the nature of the individual responsibilities of those who participated, nor is reducible to their sum total? Let us begin anew by examining an aspect of the nature of individual responsibility which can be easily overlooked. When a single person does something for which he is held solely responsible, it is generally assumed not only that such person, by his own efforts, brought about the situation for which he is being held responsible, but *that it was in his power to prevent the situation from occurring.* Now there exists a well-known class of actions in which the second condition is not met: those victimized by some inner compulsion are not generally held to be "fully" responsible for their deeds. We say that kleptomaniacs cannot prevent *themselves* from stealing. But there is a slightly different way of describing the kleptomaniac situation that reveals interesting possibilities: Kleptomaniacs, unlike ordinary persons, cannot *prevent from occurring* the robberies for which they are charged. It is not in their power to prevent them. If they could have stopped themselves from stealing, then the robberies would not have occurred. There are as well other kinds of cases in which one finds agents who cannot prevent the situations for which they are held responsible. Recently an English judge refused to send a father to jail for killing his three-year-old baby. The child was spastic and an epileptic, and had a very short life expectancy. The father pleaded guilty to manslaughter, but denied he was a murderer because nothing could prevent the early death of his baby. Of course a certain latitude has to be allowed in the description of the situation. No one can ever prevent the ultimate death of another, yet murderers cannot plead that their victims would have died sooner or later. The standard mercy killing cases do not differ from ordinary murder simply in that they are acts of mercy. It is necessary also to show that death is imminent, that no one could have postponed death for very long.

One of the more horrifying aspects of My Lai is its seeming inevitability. The ravages of a hopeless and dirty war, the incipient racism, the hatred of all Vietnamese, the moral callousness of those in charge of the war—all these factors contributed to creating, at the field operations level, a kind of soldier who could be capable of anything. To this must be added, in consideration, the standard discipline and training of any military organization, designed to produce men ready to follow orders. Given these conditions, it is important to ask who, among those who were at My Lai, could have prevented the massacre from occurring. (The entire operation was witnessed by command helicopters, and no one gave any orders to desist.) At Calley's trial a sergeant who had been at My Lai reported a soldier asking him whether he should shoot a particular old man with a beard. "If we don't kill him," the soldier said, "somebody else will." The soldier thereupon shot the old man but only wounded him; it was left to somebody else to kill him.

We like to believe that man is autonomous and cannot be compelled to do anything against his inner will. At Calley's court-martial, the prosecution pointed out that there were some at My Lai who disobeyed orders, who refused to join the slaughter. One soldier ignominiously shot himself in the foot rather than participate. (During the Second World War soldiers were instructed that *any* foot wound automatically made one liable to court-martial.) At the other end of the scale are stories of heroes who made common cause with their victims and paid the penalty. In his book, *The Warriors*, J. Glenn Gray tells of a German soldier in Holland ordered to serve on a firing squad to execute hostages. When the soldier refused to participate, he was immediately charged with treason by his superior officer, placed among the hostages, and executed on the spot.

If there are soldiers who refuse to obey repulsive orders, doesn't it show that man is really free, that every man can prevent *himself* from engaging in morally repulsive deeds? One may be optimistic about the possibilities of human freedom and still miss a crucial moral dimension here. Granted that those who participated at My Lai were not automatons but were genuinely free to act otherwise; granted that any soldier charged with murdering helpless Vietnamese could have *prevented himself* from participating in the massacre. There still remains a most important question: could any one individual at My Lai have *prevented the massacre*?

"If we don't kill him then somebody else will." Imagine that a firing squad is to be drawn from a duty roster and that no soldier relishes the assignment. In a well-run army, most soldiers will serve on firing squads if ordered to do so, though executioners are usually chosen by a call for volunteers. Suppose that everyone is uneasy about this particular execution; perhaps the victim is well liked, or it is generally believed he did not receive a fair trial or even that everyone knows he didn't commit the crime. In any event, no one volunteers to serve among the executioners. An officer decides that the most fair procedure is to draw lots. A squad of eight is randomly chosen for the firing squad and the execution takes place. Afterwards, it is ascertained that the victim was entirely innocent, that the trial was a frameup. It is now the execution squad's turn to stand trial for murder. The squad members plead that they only followed orders but it is pointed out that this is no defense, that no one is an automaton, and that all believed the victim was innocent. Perhaps a few soldiers initially chosen to serve on the squad refused to do so and suffered no dire consequences. Since no one is *compelled* to obey orders, any one on the firing squad could have prevented *himself* from committing murder. But then comes the further question: could the squad members have prevented *the murder* from taking place? This is important because it raises a different question concerning responsibility. Pointing at the squad, one can truly say: Each man is individually responsible for being among the executioners, for each could have prevented himself from being there by refusing to obey orders. However, is each member of the squad equally responsible for the execution-murder? Could any of them have prevented the execution? Is each responsible *for the execution* in exactly the same way each is responsible for being *on the squad*? An individual's refusal to serve as executioner does not prevent the execution; it only places him among those who are not criminally liable for the deed.

But among the men not criminally liable for murder are those who do share a certain responsibility, a *collective* responsibility, with the soldiers who are liable. The firing squad, remember, was selected from a duty roster, most of whom were willing to serve. Everyone on the squad knows that should he refuse someone else will take his place. "If we don't kill him somebody else will." Each squad member knows that another will be selected to take his place should he refuse. Accordingly, there is nothing *he* can do to prevent the execution. We may even imagine some strange soul among the executioners who wishes to spare the moral sensibilities of his comrades. If he refuses to serve some other unfortunate will be chosen to commit murder. As long as the class of those willing to serve on the firing squad is wider than the class of those who serve, no single individual can prevent the execution from occurring. *The collective responsible for the execution consists of the class of those who would be willing to serve on the squad if called upon to serve.* Each member of that collective shares a "collective" responsibility for the execution. Those who actually serve on the squad have, in addition to a collective responsibility, an individual responsibility, for they could have prevented themselves from serving on the squad. But no single individual in the collective can prevent the execution, when the class of those ready to act is wider than the class of actors. Potential executioners as well as executioners are linked together, for if anyone steps down there will be someone to take his place.

One may not be quite convinced. Was everyone on the large duty roster responsible in some way—a collective way—for the execution performed by a very small subset? After all, what did those who were *not* chosen really *do*? Suppose it is the genteel custom to include one blank round among the bullets distributed to the squad. No one knows beforehand whether his rifle contains the blank. The man with the blank can tell by the absence of recoil that his rifle contained a blank round, but he can only do this after he has fired, not before. Thus, only one man knows who on the squad were the "true" executioners. Suppose that the man who had the blank disclaims responsibility at the trial. He did not actually kill the victim, but only fired the blank. Is this defense credible?

Compare his case with another. Suppose, further, that one soldier in the firing squad deliberately discharged his gun into the ground. Neither he nor the man with the blank round could have caused the death of the victim. Nonetheless, one feels that there is an enormous difference between the two cases. Unlike the person who fired at the ground, the soldier with the blank *was willing to execute the victim.* He did not know when he fired if a bullet was in his gun's chamber. *He is in the same moral position as any person on the general duty roster who was willing to serve were his name to be drawn.* That is why the attempt of the man with the blank to differentiate himself from others on the squad rings hollow. All but one (the man who refused to shoot at the victim) are willing to serve as executioners. They thus share a responsibility with all members on the duty roster willing to participate if called. All share a collective responsibility for the execution-murder.

Collective Responsibility: A Moral Assessment

"If we don't kill him somebody else will." The soldier at My Lai who made that remark was saying something perfectly true, though he responded to the horrible revelation in an insane way. He was not *personally* required to shoot the old man; he was not *compelled* to kill him. But there is a certain kinship between his situation and that of the compulsive, for neither can prevent the deed for which he is liable. We excuse the compulsive because he cannot *prevent himself* from behaving in the way that he does. But it is also true that the compulsive cannot prevent *that which is done* by him. Who at My Lai could have prevented what was done there? Compulsive-like, many saw themselves forced into the executioner role which had been cast for them. Many who were not at My Lai would have been willing to do the same thing, indeed more than willing. A recent poll of a cross-section of Americans, conducted by Harvard social scientists, revealed that over half of those polled would have "shot all the inhabitants of a Vietnamese village suspected of aiding the enemy, including old men, women and children" if ordered to do so.

Can any of those who would have been willing to join Company C at My Lai be brought to trial? Other soldiers in the field, high-ranking military officers in the Pentagon, super patriots at home, any of them? All those who would have obeyed those repulsive orders at My Lai share a collective responsibility with those who were there, for without the existence of that collective, My Lai could not have happened. Nonetheless, it would be disastrous to attempt a reform of judicial procedure in order to accommodate those "collectively" responsible as well as those "individually" responsible for My Lai. The closest the law comes to dealing with collective responsibility is through the concept of conspiracy which, despite its technical complications, serves as a shotgun procedure in the hands of unscrupulous or lazy prosecutors who wish to use the evidence they have against party A to nail party B. Imagine the miscarriages of justice if one were to allow "conditional willingness" as ground for criminal liability!

Collective responsibility is a moral concept, not a legal one. The soldiers who participated at My Lai did not volunteer for that assignment. Though each soldier who took part in the massacre shoulders an individual responsibility, all were part of a much larger collective, any member of which would have gone to My Lai if ordered to do so. If you believe that My Lai would not have happened if others had been there, then the collective responsibility of those who were there is reducible to the individual responsibilities of those who took part. But if you think that replacements would have been forthcoming, then no moral assessment of My Lai can dispense with a notion of collective responsibility. If we have a special view of compulsives who cannot prevent that which they do, ought we not to extend some compassion to those who cannot prevent the deeds to which, from a mistaken sense of duty or through stupidity, they allow themselves to be attached?

KURT BAIER

Guilt and Responsibility

Who Was to Blame?

An Enemy Village, according to intelligence reports "the base camp of the experienced, tough, and long-lived 48th Viet Cong Local Force Battalion"[1] which at that time in the morning was expected to be virtually empty of non-combatants, had been made the target of one of the regular search-and-destroy missions. However, contrary to expectations, the attackers met with no resistance.[2] The people they encountered were not enemy soldiers but old men, women, children, and babies. None of them was armed, all of them perfectly cooperative. Those that had survived the preparatory bombardment and blind firing by the advancing troops were systematically rounded up, herded together, and then summarily shot.

[1] Richard Hammer, *The Court Martial of Lt. Calley* (New York: Coward, McCann & Geoghegan, 1971), p. 17.

[2] Such miscalculations appear to have occurred not infrequently. Cf. e.g. two articles by Ernest van den Haag, who investigated U.S. war crimes in Vietnam during the spring of 1971, which appeared in *National Review*, Oct. 22, esp. pp. 1171–3, and Nov. 6, 1971.

How, one wants to know, could this happen? Who was responsible for this? Who was to blame? Is it those who did the actual shooting, Lieutenant William Calley and Sergeant David Meadlo? Is it Calley and Captain Ernest Medina who gave the order to "get rid of them"? Or does the blame lie with those staff officers who conceived of the "free-fire zones" and "search-and-destroy missions" whose very aim seems to have been the destruction of all living things, including non-combatants and domestic animals? Or those who led us into this war? Is it all of us, in America and elsewhere, who support this war? Or is it all of us, irrespective of whether we are for or against it, even if we actively oppose it? Is anyone free from guilt? Or is the whole idea of pinning responsibility on someone a mistake? Is only God to blame, as was suggested by Wilbur Hamman, one of the psychiatrists called by Calley's counsel?

Calley's Guilt

In his trial Calley was formally charged with violating Article 118 of the Uniform Code of Military Justice, relating to murder. The formal charges were that at My Lai he murdered, with premeditation, not less than 107 people, including an unspecified number of women and children and one specified two-year-old. Some have argued that Calley must or should have known that his conduct was criminal. "A reasonable man, for instance, ought to know that murdering children who are only standing around is a crime even if no one has taken the trouble to explain that fact to him."[3] As an officer, he must or should have been familiar with the major provisions of the Army's Uniform Code of Military Justice and Law of Land Warfare. As an officer he also should have known the relevant portions of international law relating to war crimes, such as the Hague Convention of Land Warfare of 1907, the Nuremberg Principles laid down in 1946 in connection with the Nuremberg Trials, and the Geneva Conventions on the Laws of War of 1949.[4]

[3] Hammer, *op. cit.*, p. 10.

[4] For details concerning the law, see Arthur Everett, Kathryn Johnson, Harvey Rosenthal, *Calley* (New York: Dell Publishing Company, 1971), ch. 13 and Hammer, *op. cit.* For relevant discussions, see Richard A. Wasserstrom, ed., *War and Morality* (Belmont, California: Wadsworth, 1970) and

Thus, the Law of Land Warfare, Paragraph 2, headed *Purposes of the Law of War,* reads:

> . . . the law of land warfare . . . is inspired by the desire to diminish the evils of war by:
>
> a. Protecting both combatants and non-combatants from unnecessary suffering;
>
> b. Safeguarding certain fundamental human rights of persons who fall into the hands of the enemy, particularly prisoners of war, the wounded and sick, and civilians . . .

And paragraph 3, headed Basic Principles, reads as follows:

> a. Prohibitory Effect. The law of war places limits on the exercise of a belligerent's power in the interests mentioned in paragraph 2 and requires that belligerents refrain from employing any kind or degree of violence which is not actually necessary for military purposes and that they conduct hostilities with regard for the principles of humanity and chivalry.
>
> The prohibitory effect of the law of war is not minimized by "military necessity" which has been defined as that principle which justifies those measures *not forbidden by international law* [my italics] which are indispensable for securing the complete submission of the enemy as soon as possible. Military necessity has been generally rejected as a defense for acts forbidden by the customary and conventional laws of war inasmuch as the latter have been developed and framed with consideration for the concept of military necessity.

Article 3 of The Geneva Conventions on the Laws of War states:

> . . . (1) Persons taking no active part in the hostilities, including members of armed forces who have laid down their arms and those placed *hors de combat* by sickness, wounds, *detention* [my italics], or any other cause, shall in all circumstances be treated humanely, without any adverse distinction founded on race, color, religion, faith, . . . To this end, the following acts are and shall remain prohibited at any time and in any place whatsoever with respect to the above-mentioned persons:
>
> (a) violence to life and person, in particular murder of all kinds, mutilation, cruel treatment, and torture. . . .

Richard A. Wasserstrom. "The relevance of Nuremburg," *Philosophy and Public Affairs* (Fall, 1971).

Calley's conduct, at least in the two mass shootings, constituted what the reasonable man should know were moral wrongs. They also constituted a violation of the "fundamental human rights of persons who fall into the hands of the enemy, particularly . . . civilians," as required by Article 2 of the U. S. Law of Land Warfare and by Article 3 of the Geneva Conventions on the Laws of War. Therefore, being forbidden equally by U.S. and international law, such conduct could not be justified even by military necessity. In any case, there was no such necessity.

Calley, however, was also required to obey lawful superior orders. He claimed that the briefings by Captain Medina given officers and troops on the eve of the attack on My Lai were to destroy all living things, including women, children, and domestic animals. Though denied by Medina, some other soldiers claimed to have interpreted the briefing in this way. Whatever Medina's actual words, the briefing was given at a time when Intelligence reports suggested that the village was the base of a V. C. company and had been evacuated by civilians. The incorrectness of this information became obvious soon after the occupation of My Lai, and an officer should have been able to take this into account in his interpretation of the instructions. However, Calley also claimed that during the operation Medina issued the specific order "to get rid of" the people he had rounded up—"to waste them." Medina denied giving this order, but it is not improbable that Calley interpreted his words in this way. We shall therefore assume that Calley believed, and indeed had adequate reason to believe, that he was given the order to kill all living things including the civilians in the village. What bearing does that have on whether he was guilty as charged?

The Law of Land Warfare, section 509, headed *Defense of Superior Orders,* has this to say:

> a. The fact that the law of war has been violated pursuant to an order of a superior authority, whether military or civil, does not deprive the act in question of its character as a war crime nor does it constitute a defense in the trial of an accused individual, unless he did not know and could not reasonably have been expected to know that the act was unlawful. In all cases where the order is held not to constitute a defense to an allegation of war crime, the fact that

> the individual was acting pursuant to orders may be considered in mitigation of punishment.
>
> b. In considering the question of whether a superior order constitutes a valid defense, the court shall take into consideration the fact that obedience to lawful military orders is the duty of every member of the armed forces; that the latter cannot be expected, in conditions of war discipline, to weigh scrupulously the legal merits of the order received; that certain rules of warfare may be controversial; or that an act otherwise amounting to a war crime may be done in obedience to orders conceived as a measure of reprisal. *At the same time it must be borne in mind that members of the armed forces are bound to obey only lawful orders.* [my italics]

Counsel for Calley, in his opening address, spoke of the "resentment and anger . . . engendered in the minds and hearts of the survivors by the means and methods used by the enemy. The use of mines, booby traps, sniper fire, and ambushes aided by civilians of all ages and sexes had taken its toll."[5] Thus it seemed he wished to construe Calley's acts as "Reprisals." On this subject the Army Field Manual on the Law of Land Warfare says:

> . . . Reprisals against the persons or property of prisoners of war, including the wounded and sick, and protected civilians, are forbidden. Collective penalties and punishment of prisoners of war and protected civilians are likewise prohibited. . . . Reprisals are never adopted merely for revenge, but only as an unavoidable last resort to induce the enemy to desist from unlawful practices. They should never be employed by individual soldiers except by direct orders of a commander, and the latter should give such orders only after careful inquiry into the alleged offense.

According to military regulations, then, an order such as the one given to Calley was unlawful and therefore not binding on him. Even if Medina gave that order, this would not exonerate Calley. An order to do something unlawful cannot make doing it lawful; even an authorized superior cannot obligate one to obey it.

Still, Calley could advance two other excuses. He might claim that although he knew the order to be unlawful, he considered it too dangerous to risk "such disobedience in the face of the

[5] Hammer, *op. cit.*, p. 178.

enemy." In other words, though he did not think that what he did was justified, he could claim that he could not have been expected to take the risk involved in doing what was right. In the circumstances this would be a very weak excuse indeed, for several others (e.g. Conti and Dursi) refused the very same orders in the face of the enemy. Calley, who was not even near Medina when he claimed to have received the order, cannot therefore have had any genuine apprehension about what would happen to him if he disobeyed.

The other excuse would be to say that he regarded Medina's order as legal and binding because he did not see anything seriously wrong in killing large numbers of Vietnamese non-combatants, including children and babies, since that was a necessary part of what was, after all, described as a "search and destroy" mission. Concerning this excuse Colonel Kennedy, the judge in the Calley trial, instructed the jury as follows:

> A determination that an order is illegal does not, of itself, assign criminal responsibility to the person following the order for acts done in compliance with it. Soldiers are taught to follow orders and special attention is given to obedience of orders on the battlefield. Military effectiveness depends on obedience to orders. On the other hand, the obedience of a soldier is not the obedience of an automaton. A soldier is a reasoning agent, obliged to respond, not as a machine, but as a person. The law takes these factors into account in assessing criminal responsibility for acts done in compliance with illegal orders. The acts of a subordinate done in compliance with an unlawful order given him by his superior are excused and impose no criminal liability upon him unless the superior's order is one which a man of ordinary sense and understanding would, under the circumstances, know to be unlawful, or if the order in question is actually known to the accused to be unlawful.[6]

Thus, to be guilty as charged, Calley must be "criminally responsible." He is criminally responsible if Medina did not give the order in question, if Calley believed that the order was unlawful, or if a reasonable man in the circumstances would have known it. It did not become clear beyond reasonable doubt that Medina did not give the order in question or that Calley did not

[6] Everett, et al., *op. cit.*, pp. 206–207.

have adequate reason to think that he was under such orders, or, for that matter, that Calley believed these orders were unlawful.

But is it fair to say that Calley was "criminally responsible" simply on the grounds that a "man of ordinary sense and understanding" would have known that the order was unlawful? Surely a person should be declared criminally responsible only if he *should* have known that such an order was unlawful. But from the fact that a man of ordinary sense and understanding *would* have known, it does not follow that every type of person *should* have known. If Calley was not a person of that type—and much of the psychiatric evidence produced during the trial cast doubt on whether he was—then it would be necessary to show, in addition, either that it was Calley's fault (not someone else's) that he was not such a person, or that he should have known better, even though he was not such a person. No such evidence was produced. Indeed, in view of the evidence that he was not a reasonable person and the lack of evidence to show that this was his fault, the available evidence tends to place the blame for this ignorance elsewhere. Considering the difficulty of the task of deciding whether an order is lawful or not, officers surely ought to be thoroughly instructed in such problems. Calley's account of his training, however, shows it to have been not only perfunctory but even quite misleading. Calley testified that "all orders were to be assumed legal, that the soldier's job was to carry out any order given him to the best of his ability" and that "if I had questioned an order, I was supposed to carry the order out and then come back and make my complaint."[7] Perhaps a "reasonable" person would have seen through this teaching, but Calley appears to have accepted it at face value. A society prepared to turn men like Calley into officers incurs an additional responsibility to make clear to them the distinctions they are supposed to draw particularly if society seriously intends later to charge them with failure to do so.

The Army's reluctance to press charges of atrocities or war crimes, together with the perfunctoriness of its instructions in what are war crimes and its pursuit of policies involving "free fire zones" and "search-and-destroy missions," may well have

[7] Cf. Hammer, *op. cit.*, pp. 240 ff.

created in Calley and others a conviction that the Army was not taking its own rules on war crimes very seriously or did not view these activities in its own definition of war crimes.[8]

If Colonel Kennedy was right in his interpretation of "criminal responsibility" (and there is no doubt that this is a correct interpretation of the law), then Calley really was guilty of murder as charged. If doubts remain about this interpretation of "criminal responsibility," then equally there is doubt about Calley's guilt as charged.

GUILT AND RESPONSIBILITY

Even if Calley is criminally responsible in the sense explained, does this show that he is responsible for My Lai? Does it show that he is solely responsible for it? It seems not. The question "Who is responsible for My Lai?" is not the same question as "Who is guilty of murdering people at My Lai?" The statement that "Calley was guilty of murdering people at My Lai" does not mean or even imply that "Calley is responsible for murdering people at My Lai." A person may well be "guilty but insane" but could hardly be "responsible but insane." If he were insane, he would not be "responsible for (any of) his actions" and so could not be responsible for murder. A person may be guilty of committing a crime, as perhaps Fagin's boys were of thieving, yet somebody else may be responsible for the crime, that is, for *their* committing it. Whatever Fagin was guilty of, and whatever the children were responsible for, it was not thieving; yet the children were guilty of thieving, and it was *their* thieving that Fagin was responsible for. Similarly, from the fact that Calley was guilty of murdering these civilians, it does not follow that he was responsible for murdering them, since someone else may be responsible for *his* murdering them. At the same time, the fact that Calley was guilty of murdering these people does not mean that he is *not* responsible for murdering them either: his guilt is compatible with both his responsibility and his non-responsibility. Even if others are responsible for *his* murdering them, it may still be true that he, too, is responsible for murdering them.

[8] Cf. the report on war crimes by Ernest van den Haag in *National Review* (Oct. 22 and Nov. 6, 1971, pp. 1172–3, 1128–1231).

Determining who is guilty of a certain act is thus quite a different matter from determining who is responsible for it. "Guilty of something" does not mean the same thing as "Responsible for something." Moreover, the "something" in question is never the same type of thing. "Who is guilty of X?" can be asked only about doings, and only about the agent's doings at that, never about events. "Who is responsible for Y?" can be asked only about events, never about doings. "Who is responsible for doing X yesterday?" is simply not a well-formed question.[9]

This last point is easily overlooked because other similar questions are perfectly in order, such as "Who is responsible for Smith's doing X yesterday?" or "Is Smith responsible for doing X yesterday?" We can ask these two questions because they make clear that we are inquiring into the responsibility for Smith's doing X yesterday and that we leave open the question of whether the person responsible is Smith or someone else. By contrast, the question "Who is responsible for doing X yesterday?" implies that the subject of the sentence refers to the person doing X. "Smith is responsible for doing X yesterday" implies that the action Smith is responsible for is *his* doing X. The question "Who is responsible for doing X yesterday?" thus implies the false assumption that the person who did X *must* also be responsible for doing X.[10]

[9] 'Who is responsible for supplies?' is a well-formed question, but only because it does not inquire into responsibility for something particular which has already happened, but inquires into what I call "(task-) responsibility."

[10] For the benefit of those interested in recent discussions of this topic, I should say that this appears to be the oversight which led Hart into saying that with utterances such as "He did it" (e.g. "He hit her") "we *confess* or *admit* liability, make accusations, or *ascribe* responsibility." (H. L. A. Hart, "The Ascription of Responsibility and Rights," *Proceedings of the Aristotelian Society* 1948–1949. Section III.) "He did it" never ascribes responsibility for something: when the vase lies broken on the floor, "He did it" may well ascribe responsibility for "it," the vase's having been smashed. But "He hit her" is not a suitable substitute for "He did it," because it contains no "it" for which this remark can by implication ascribe responsibility to the hitter. "He did it" can simultaneously do two jobs: identify a doer of an unspecified doing implied to be relevantly related to "it" and ascribe responsibility for "it" (not the doing) to the doer. "He hit her" can do only one job, namely, identify the hitter. It must leave open the question of

THE CONCEPT OF RESPONSIBILITY

What, then, is this further question we raise when we inquire into whether a person who has done something, who may even be guilty of a certain crime or act of wrong-doing, is responsible for it and perhaps for other things as well? We can quickly dispose of the claim that, since the non-combatants were killed by projectiles from weapons fired by Calley, he himself must be responsible for these deaths and so for the worst outrages at My Lai. If this were true, then the gunners in the artillery and the advancing troops firing into the village must be equally responsible, and so must their bullets and their weapons. But from having been physically responsible for executing the firings and the destruction, it does not follow that all these men, let alone the projectiles and the weapons, should be *held* responsible for their actions and the resultant deaths. What, then, is the difference? When is it true that if a person is responsible for

---

who is responsible for his hitting her: it may not be he at all but his guardian, or she may have only herself to blame.

The same mistake is made by Joel Feinberg, *Doing and Deserving* (Princeton, N.J.: Princeton University Press, 1970), pp. 137–139, who argues, quite correctly, that Hart did not, after all, make a mistake when he said that "He hit her" can be "ascriptive," for "sometimes we have the action, so to speak, in our hands, and we want to know . . . whom to pin it on." (*Ibid.*, p. 137.) Feinberg is, however, wrong in thinking that *ascribing an action* to someone is *ascribing responsibility* for the action to him. It is false to say that "'It was Mary who smiled' ascribes the responsibility *for smiling* to Mary." (*Ibid.*, 139.) "It was Mary who smiled" cannot simultaneously ascribe to Mary the action of smiling and the responsibility for that action. When we want to ascribe a deed to someone by identifying him as the doer, what we "have in our hands" is only a *type* of action, *smiling,* something that is not a particular action until it is "pinned down" to some agent. When we want to ascribe responsibility for some action to someone, what we must have in our hands is a particular action, something already pinned down to some agent. This does not of course mean that we must know the agent's name or anything else about him. We may ask who is responsible for the killings of certain people by unknown killers, but even then the question is not about the identity of the killers. (When the Yablonski killers will have been identified, we shall know who killed the Yablonskis, we shall know who is guilty of those killings, but we still may not know who is responsible for these killings, for these killers' killing of the Yablonskis.)

something it is appropriate to hold him responsible for it; when not?

Explanatory and Practical Points of View. The difference in interpreting responsibility is tied to differences between two types of practical points of view. Looking for who or what is responsible is an activity conducted from one of these points of view. By contrast, when we seek understanding or explanation of something, we have a different point of view.

Thus suppose that, during a prolonged trip abroad, Jones undergoes a vasectomy without telling his wife. A year after his return his wife becomes pregnant. He could understand this on the assumption that she was unfaithful to him. If he has enough evidence to dismiss this explanation, he still cannot understand her pregnancy if his model of what happens after vasectomy leads him to believe that it is impossible for him to impregnate her. He does not understand what has happened until he has a clearer grasp or picture or model of what is involved in vasectomy. Jones may not, however, be satisfied with merely understanding the pregnancy of his wife. When he asks who or what was responsible for that pregnancy, he implies that he is speaking from a practical, not merely an explanatory, point of view. He implies that he is looking for something, control of which would enable one to produce or prevent such impregnations by vasectomized males.

Causal and Agent Responsibility. The individual practical point of view from which we sometimes raise questions of responsibility is that of an individual who confronts his environment with a view to tampering with it for his personal ends. From such a point of view, the events to be expected naturally divide into those wanted and those unwanted by the individual, and the information he seeks is in the nature of "know-how," telling him what he must or can do to bring about wanted events and to prevent unwanted events. Such general know-how can be couched in terms of responsibility. Thus the notion that "faulty brake linings, icy roads, and poor construction of steering mechanisms *are* responsible for car accidents" implies that any person who regards car accidents as undesirable and so desires to prevent them must be sure to have good brake linings and to avoid icy roads and cars with faulty steering. In saying that a faulty brake lining *was* responsible for some accident which has already occurred, one is simply applying such general knowledge to a particular case. When we adopt this point of view, then, we pick out as responsible for something those things which we, the users of the information, will want to modify in order to prevent events unwanted or bring about events wanted by us. No thought is given to the permissibility or otherwise of tampering with the things responsible, or about doing something to rectify the situation brought about by the responsible factor. We can indicate responsibility ascriptions from this point of view by the expression "(causal) responsibility."

In a social application the practical point of view can be that of a member of an organized group bent on tampering with the environment as a collective agent in order to improve upon it. By their behavior any number of the members of such a group are or can be factors contributing to the coming about of wanted or unwanted events which would not come about otherwise—that is, if they behaved differently or were not there at all—or to the prevention of such events which otherwise would come about. From the point of view of a member of such a community, it is therefore a much more intricate business to determine what must be changed if unwanted events are to be prevented and wanted events to be brought about. In our society this involves the following important social practices and institutions.

First, we lay down for our society as a whole the considerations on the basis of which certain sorts of events are to be regarded as wanted and others as unwanted ("socially wanted-unwanted"), quite independently of whether they are wanted or unwanted from the point of view of this or that person. Thus the pollution of a given privately owned stream by an industry in the neighborhood is unwanted from the stream-owner's, though not from the industrialist's, point of view; it may be wanted or unwanted from the society's point of view, depending upon the relative importance to it of the industry's product and of the cleanness of the stream.

Next, we make clear (in ways described below) what each person *must* do or not do towards bringing about the most important socially wanted events and preventing the socially unwanted events. We can call this procedure "assigning to each his responsibility to society." This by implication also tells the individual what he or she may and may not do towards bringing about personally wanted events and preventing personally unwanted events. Thus if pollution of a certain stream is socially unwanted, then the industrialist may not continue manufacturing his product which he personally wants if this involves polluting that stream.

Another thing we make clear in our society is what measures may or will be taken against those individuals who do not discharge their responsibility to society. We can call this "society's responsibility to the wronged." Such measures include punishment, compulsory medical, psychiatric, or reformative treatment, and compulsory indemnification of those who have incurred loss, damage, injury, harm, or suffering as a result of a person's failing to discharge his responsibility to society.

Finally, we assign to appropriate authorities the task of taking rectifying measures when unwanted events do occur or wanted events do not occur. I shall call this "society's responsibility to the unfortunate." It has become plain in recent years that making the individual who is responsible for the damage pay for it may not protect members of the society from unwanted events as effectively as arranging, say, for compulsory insurance. Once the primitive idea is given up that all socially unwanted events are to be blamed on some agent, we are more ready to consider other and more bountiful sources from which the unfortunate and the wronged may derive relief.[11]

From the individual practical point of view, then, we can ascribe responsibility "(causal) responsibility" to events (explosions, collapses), things (gas furnaces, houses), or persons (repair men, residents), but we cannot say that these things were responsible *to someone,* nor that they should be *held* (except in the innocuous sense of *"considered"* or *"believed to be"*) responsible. From this point of view, we can say only that a person *was* responsible for something that has already happened, not that he *is* responsible for it. Such responsibility cannot be *assigned* or

[11] For arguments against this approach, see e.g. Ernest van den Haag, *op. cit.*, pp. 1176, 1227–1228, 1232.

assumed or otherwise *acquired*. We can assign responsibility only to persons: only persons who have had the sort of responsibility for something which can be assigned can later be *held* responsible for something that happened, and then only if its happening shows that they failed in their assigned, assumed, or otherwise acquired responsibility; and only persons who have failed in this responsibility can *be* responsible for something that has happened.

Despite the greater number of things one can say about responsibility from the social rather than from the individual practical point of view, *ascribing responsibility* to an x for something y that has already happened, comes to the same thing in both cases, namely, singling out an x which satisfies these two conditions: (1) x has a property, φ, such that the event y would not have happened in those (normal) circumstances in which it did happen if x had not possessed φ; (2) when we want to prevent (or reduce the likelihood of) the recurrence of events of the same type as y, then, of all the things with properties like y in the respect specified in (1), it is x which it is best, all things considered, to change so that it no longer has the property φ. Of course, the grounds on which a given x can be said to satisfy condition (2) will be very different when ascribing responsibility from these two different practical points of view. The most obvious differences concern the status of x, the characteristic φ on account of which x can have responsibility ascribed to it, and the way in which any properties of x may legitimately be changed to produce the desired result. When we adopt the social practical point of view, we employ many safeguards to protect those to be declared and later held responsible. Nobody can have responsibility for some past occurrence ascribed to him unless that occurrence can be attributed to a failure in his responsibility to society, that is, his failure in a task he could have performed and knew he was required to perform; he cannot be held responsible for it except by persons to whom he was responsible for his failure; he can be subjected to corrective measures only if he failed to give a satisfactory answer when held responsible; and there are only certain carefully circumscribed forms of corrective measures to which he may be subjected, for the sake of ensuring that he will not bring about socially unwanted events or prevent socially wanted ones, or for the sake of rectifying states he has already brought about.

In considering ascriptions of responsibility from the social, practical point of view, we need to avoid confusion by distinguishing "causal responsibility" and "agent-responsibility," though most of the time it will not be necessary to add this qualification. This explains why we want to say that the artillery gunners, the blindly firing infantry, Meadlo and Calley—but not Medina—were responsible, that is, (causally) responsible, for the deaths of many civilians; but the gunners, the infantry men and perhaps Meadlo are not, whereas Calley and perhaps Medina are, responsible, that is (agent-) responsible, for these deaths. The question now arises how we would answer these latter questions.

The Dimensions of (Agent-) Responsibility. This type of responsibility involves at least two persons, the person *who* is responsible for something and the person *to whom* he is responsible. The former has a certain task to perform, which I shall call his "(task-) responsibility"—what he is "(task-) responsible for." Performing that task is discharging, not performing it is failing in, his (task-) responsibility. The person to whom he is (task-) responsible also has a task, namely, to *supervise* the person who is (task-) responsible to him, or to *hold him responsible* when he is failing in his (task-) responsibility. This task may in turn be a (task-) responsibility for which the second person is (task-) responsible to a third and so on, till we come to someone who is thus (task-) responsible to society, as is the Commander-in-Chief of the Armed Forces or the Board of Trustees of a State University. But there need be no such chain of responsibility: everyone of us is (task-) responsible directly to society for a lot of things, such as ensuring that our taxes get paid.

Holding a person responsible consists of making him give an account of how he has handled his task responsibility. If he has discharged it, then no more needs to be done. If he has failed to discharge it, then he is responsible for the failure; that is, he must answer why he failed. We can say in such a case that he is "(answerable-) responsible" for it. Suppose the placement officer of a department is the person (task-) responsible to the department for getting students placed; then he is (answerable-) responsible to the department for students *not* getting placed, that is for his failure to get them placed. That he is (answerable-) responsible means that he must explain why he failed and that, to be in the clear, he must give an exonerating, exculpating or, at least excusing answer. If the explanation is inculpating, then his failure is culpable, he *is* "(culpable-) responsible" for his failure. The task of *holding him* responsible for his failure then proceeds to the next step, the taking of appropriate rectifying measures by the person to whom he is responsible: perhaps dressing him down, admonishing, reprimanding, warning him, perhaps even firing or punishing him.[12]

It is now clear why we think that the gunners and infantry men are not, while Meadlo, Calley, and Medina may well be, (agent-) responsible for the deaths of these non-combatants; we are inclined to think the former did not, while the latter did, fail in their (task-) responsibility; the first group did discharge their responsibility to society, while the second group did not.

Our (Task-) Responsibility. How, then do we become (task-) responsible? There seem to be three different ways: deliberately *assuming* responsibility, as when Jones' brother, after the death of Jones and his wife in a plane crash, assumes responsibility for the orphaned children; or being *saddled with* responsibility by the circumstances, as when the oldest son is saddled with the responsibility for his siblings after his parents' death; or having responsibility *assigned* to one, as when a court assigns responsibility for the orphaned children to an official guardian. But in the end, all three ways are dependent on society's authority to determine how individuals come to have (task-) responsibility.

If we accept these observations about the social, practical point of view which underlies the idea of (agent-) responsibility, then it is easy to see what must be the principle underlying society's methods of allocating (task-) responsibility to its members. It must be to modify their natural behavior patterns with a view to reducing the number of socially unwanted events and increasing the number of socially wanted events. In our society we

[12] Those who desire a fuller account may consult H. L. A. Hart, *Punishment and Responsibility* (New York: Oxford University Press, 1968), esp. Ch. IX. My views can be found in two articles: Richard T. DeGeorge, ed., "Responsibility and Freedom, *Ethics and Society* (New York: Doubleday, 1966), pp. 48–84 and Myles Brand, ed. "Responsibility and Action," *The Nature of Human Action* (New York: Scott-Foresman, 1970), pp. 100–116.

employ two simple ways and a more sophisticated one for accomplishing this end. The first includes spelling out and prohibiting certain modes of behavior: those which necessarily aim at certain socially unwanted events, whether these aims are reached, as in the case of murder, or whether they are not, as in the case of attempted murder; and those which, like driving above certain speed limits, do not necessarily involve aiming at socially unwanted events but nevertheless frequently bring them about. This first method also includes spelling out and requiring certain other modes of behavior: those which prevent unwanted events from occurring, such as helping another person in need when the need is urgent and when one is in a good position to offer help. The second method involves the setting up of certain minimal standards of circumspection, caution, forethought, and care, concerning the accidental or unintended bringing about or prevention of certain socially wanted or unwanted events, and then requiring of everyone that in his own activities he observe these minimal standards of care. The point of this is that observation of these standards would increase the incidence of wanted and diminish that of unwanted events, while ignoring them would have the opposite effect.

The third and more sophisticated method differs from the first two in that it not merely imposes certain *curbs* on people's natural aims, for the sake of thereby preventing some events and bringing about others, but makes it the prime role of certain persons to devote their energy, knowledge, skills, and ingenuity to the task of bringing about socially wanted and preventing socially unwanted events. The function of the police, for instance, is not merely to help in carrying out the task of bringing to account those who have already failed in their responsibility under the first two heads, but also by their presence to deter and perhaps forcibly stop some who in their absence might well proceed to do so.

Calley's Responsibility

What was Calley responsible *for*? He was found guilty of murder, but this implies only that he intentionally did something he should have known was a crime. If he had had a mental disease adversely affecting his ability to judge and choose, he would not have been "responsible for his acts," *any* of his acts; he would have been not "accountable," and so not *responsible for* committing the criminal acts he was found *guilty of* committing. However, he was found not to have had such a mental disease and so he was responsible for committing these crimes.[13] Since his murders involve the deaths of non-combatants, he is also responsible for these deaths. What does this come to?

That he is responsible for committing these crimes implies that he satisfies all the conditions for the proper application to him of "retributive" measures designed to rectify in a certain way the disturbance brought about by his crimes. Retributive measures, as we understand this term, are those measures to be applied to a person when he has failed in that most important part of his responsibility to society which specifies what socially undesirable events he must not aim at and what standards of care he must not fall below. They are designed to bring home to him the error of his ways and to bring about a change. Punishment is often said to serve this end, though it is doubtful whether it actually does. By contrast, that Calley is responsible for *the deaths* of these people only implies that he satisfies all the conditions for applying to him a different type of rectifying measures, namely, those designed to restore conditions as far as possible to those prevailing before these deaths. I shall say that when a person satisfies either of these two sets of conditions, he is "(liable-) responsible." Both these uses of "(liability-) responsibility" imply that the rectifying measures to be taken would be at the expense of someone whose fault it was that conditions need restoring to an earlier superior level.

Individual and Group Responsibility

The question now arises, however, whether Calley alone was guilty of murder and he alone (liable-) responsible for the deaths of non-combatants; and whether he was the chief culprit. Are not other individuals more blameworthy? Did not others bear a greater share of the responsibility? Were we not all of us collectively responsible? But then again, does it even make sense to say that one man is responsible for what another does? Is not this as

[13] Hammer, *op. cit.*, ch. 16.

confused an idea as getting rid of one's guilt by killing a scapegoat? And are there really degrees of responsibility? Must we not say, rather, that a person is either responsible for something or he is not, and not that he has a certain higher or lower degree of responsibility for it?

Degrees and Other Dimensions of Responsibility. Let us note, in passing, that it is misleading to think of guilt as having degrees. "He is guilty" means "He committed the act," that is, the act of which he is accused. He can only be either guilty or not guilty, not more or less so. Of course, there are different degrees of intensity of a person's guilt feelings, that is, the feelings experienced by the average person when he or she acknowledges the justice of an accusation against him. When two people guilty of the same thing have guilt feelings of different intensity, we can say that one "feels guiltier" than the other. When it is also appropriate for one to have stronger guilt feelings than the other, we want to infer that one must be guiltier than the other. This is misleading, however, since it is a conflation of four different matters: the "magnitude of the guilt," i.e. of the crime; the "degree of culpability," i.e. the measure of available extenuations and aggravations; the "degree of blameworthiness," which is a function of the first two; and the "extent of his (liability-) responsibility," which is a function of many things. Thus, Meadlo and Calley were both guilty of murders on a large scale; hence the magnitude of their crimes was much the same. But Meadlo *felt* a lot guiltier though he was less culpable than Calley, since he acted on repeated and insistent orders by a superior officer standing over him and since he was less qualified than Calley to judge the lawfulness of these orders. Meadlo therefore was less blameworthy than Calley, and the extent of his (liability-) responsibility was more limited than Calley's.

But are there really degrees of responsibility? Was Calley more responsible for the deaths for which *he* was responsible than Meadlo for those deaths for which *he* was responsible? Was Calley *very* responsible for them and Meadlo only *a little* or *mildly* so? Or are there no degrees of responsibility?

Here we must distinguish between the various uses of "responsibility" already distinguished: "accountability" (as in "Calley was responsible for his actions"), "(task-) responsibility," "(answerability-) responsibility," and "(liability-) responsibility." There are degrees of accountability: in this sense a person may have full or only diminished responsibility or none at all. A person's diminished responsibility altogether exempts him from (task-) responsibility for certain things or creates excuses for failure in certain (task-) responsibilities. By contrast, it does not make sense to speak of degrees of (task-) responsibility or (answerability-) responsibility though, as we have seen, it does make sense to speak of degrees of (culpability-) responsibility. Lastly, we cannot speak of degrees of (liability-) responsibility, but we can think of one person's (liability-) responsibility as greater than another's because he is liable *to* a greater burden than the other. Thus when we compare people's responsibility "in magnitude" we must remember that it is (accountability-) responsibility and (culpability-) responsibility that vary in degree, (task-) responsibility and (answerability-) responsibility that vary in extent, and (liability-) responsibility that varies in the magnitude of the burden.

External and Internal Responsibility. In the case of (task-) responsibility we can, however, think of responsibility *as shared* equally or unequally, among a number of people. Hence, though there is no question of the degree of (task-) responsibility or (answerability-) responsibility or (liability-) responsibility, there is a question of one's share in the total responsibility for that for which one is, together with others, responsible. We can, in such a case, speak of "joint responsibility." The members of an appointments committee may have joint responsibility for making appointments, each member bearing an equal share of that responsibility. Let us call this the committee's "external responsibility." When the committee fails in its external (task-) responsibility, then it is (answerable-) responsible to certain persons and can be held responsible for this failure by the person(s) *to whom* it is responsible, say, the Senate. If the committee has no chairman, then each member has an equal share in the common tasks. Call that a member's "internal responsibility." If a member can show that he has discharged his internal (task-) responsibility, then he is not (liable-) responsible for, does not bear any share in the (liability-) responsibility for, the Committee's failure in its external (task-) responsibility. Where the committee has a chairman, the external responsibility is usually divided up among its members in different and unequal ways, the chairman taking a much heavier load of the (task-) responsibility than the others as well as being solely (answerable-) responsible for the committee's failure. However, the members are internally (answerable-) responsible to the chairman. Thus when such a committee fails in its (task-) responsibility, it is the chairman who is answerable to the Senate, and he will therefore attempt to prevent failure by overseeing the members' work.

A chairman is thus "responsible for" the members of the committee in that he is held responsible for those failures of the committee which are failures in the internal responsibilities of its members. It is therefore desirable that he should have authority to direct its members, perhaps power to discipline them if necessary.

When we speak of "being responsible for Jones," we mean being a group member (answerable-) and/or (liable-) responsible for any failure in Jones' internal (task-) responsibility, and usually also being (task-) responsible for seeing to it that Jones discharges his internal responsibility. Masters are in this way responsible *for* their servants, officers *for* their subordinates, and the represented *for* their representatives. Of course, guardians of insane wards are not (task-) responsible for getting their wards to discharge their internal responsibility, for such wards do not have any. Such guardians have all the external responsibility, and, since there are only two members in this group and one of them is not accountable, no one has any internal responsibility at all.

In some complex groups, such as the army, church, corporation, or trade union, whose structures involve a hierarchical chain of responsibility for subordinates, we find a corresponding hierarchical chain of authority over the subordinates. In such groups everyone is responsible *to* his superior and responsible *for* his subordinate. In such a group, the chief bears external (answerability-) responsibility for the group's failure in its (task-) responsibility. Members of such groups are not, however, completely protected from external (answerability-) and (liability-) responsibility. The chief need not take the rap for all their failures. He can, by an investigation of the behavior of his subordinates, place the (culpability-) responsibility and so the external (liability-) responsibility on some person lower down in the hierarchy if he can show that he himself, and the commanders between him and that person can show that they themselves, discharged their internal (task-) responsibility. Thus the question of who was responsible for the slaughter at My Lai is essentially the question of whether or not Meadlo, Calley, Medina, and the officers above them failed in their internal (task-) responsibility. If Meadlo need not but Calley ought to have known that the order Calley claimed to have been given by Medina and passed on to Meadlo was unlawful, then Meadlo did but Calley did not discharge his internal (task-) responsibility. Hence Meadlo does not, but Calley does, bear a share in the external (liability-) responsibility for the slaughter. If Medina gave the order to "waste" the men, then he too failed in his internal (task-) responsibility; and, as mentioned before, those who are (task-) responsible for officer training may be said to have failed in their internal (task-) responsibility for enlightening officers on what are war crimes and what are unlawful orders. Again, those who conceived of "free fire zones" and "search-and-destroy" operations may well have failed in their internal (task-) responsibility if these strategic concepts involve the certainty or high risk of killings and devastations which are contrary to international law. If so, then these persons, who have failed in their internal (task-) responsibility, also bear some part, perhaps even a large part, of the external (liability-) responsibility for My Lai.

THE SOVEREIGN PEOPLE

A further extension of responsibility occurs in societies which are democratic. For in such societies, unlike those which, for instance, subscribe to the "Divine Right of Kings," it is the people who are "sovereign." This sets up a new supreme authority to which the government is construed as being internally responsible, though it is one to which it is notoriously difficult to give institutional form. Thus, in a democratic society the members play two quite different and opposed roles, and so does the government. While as subjects the members of the society occupy the lowest rank in the political order, as sovereign they "collectively" occupy the highest rank and are therefore responsible *for* its subordinates, including the government and its organs. While as ruler of its subjects the government occupies the highest rank of the political order, as servant, representative, or agent of the sovereign body of citizens it is subordinate and responsible to that sovereign.[14]

When speaking of "group responsibility," we must therefore make distinctions among three types of cases: those cases in which it is a group (such as the German people or the Waffen SS, or the U. S. army) which is held responsible *for* the acts of certain individuals; those cases in which it is certain individuals (such as Hitler or the Commander-in-Chief) who are held responsible *for* the acts of a group, such as a country's declaration of war, an army's invasion of a country, or a battalion's preparatory artillery barrage; and those cases in which a group (such as a business or a church) is held responsible for the acts of another group (such as an organization of watchmen or a university).

The final question concerns cases of the last kind. It is simply the question of whether we, the American people, the sovereign, should conceive ourselves as being "collectively" responsible, that is, externally (answerable-) responsible, to some potential tribunal, such as that which was set up at Nuremberg after World War II, and (liable-) responsible for the massacre at My Lai.[15]

We are considering the question of the external responsibility of one group, American civilians, for the acts of another group and its members, the American army. We have already noted that the Army's chief is (answerable-) responsible to the government for failures in the (task-) responsibility of the Army, but that he can escape (liability-) responsibility for such failures in the internal (task-) responsibility of his men if he can show that he discharged his internal (task-) responsibility. Now, if we are as a group (answerable-) responsible for our government and for the Army it uses to carry out its policies, then all of us are—as a group, not individually—(answerable-) responsible for failures in the

[14] Cf. Jean Lacques Rousseau, *Social Contract,* Bk. 1, Chs. VI, VII.

[15] I ignore the fact that there is not now such a tribunal, just as the Allies then ignored the fact that there was no such tribunal when the crimes were committed.

Army's (task-) responsibility. It seems, then, that one could justifiably maintain that we are so responsible, for the government is internally (answerable-) responsible to us, the sovereign. Because we sit in judgment on its policies at election time, it is easier and less risky for us than for members of most other kinds of societies to convey to the government our criticism of its policies.

Suppose, then, that we really are in this way "collectively" (task-) responsible for ensuring that governmental policies are morally acceptable, that various sections of the Army, including several officers of Charlie Company and others, were (liable-) responsible for these massacres; that unlike the Army brass who have demonstrated that they have not failed in their (task-) responsibility, "we" are all externally answerable for these individual failures which jointly produced the Army's failure in one of its (task-) responsibilities, namely, the prevention of war crimes. Given all this, what was the internal (task-) responsibility of each member whose discharge constituted the discharge of *his share* of the sovereign's external (task-) responsibility for the prevention of war crimes? Those who have protested against the war or its more obnoxious strategies, those who have engaged in acts of civil disobedience, or those who have become conscientious objectors, have surely done much towards discharging that internal responsibility. Even those who have supported the war have not, of course, *ipso facto* failed in their internal responsibility, for supporting a war is not the same as sharing in the responsibility for war crimes.

Who, then, has failed? No doubt there are many ways in which one can fail. Let us simply take an example. Let us assume that there is a certain attitude towards the lives of others, particularly those of other cultures, which is not uncommon among soldiers anywhere, and that, under the sort of pressure to which Calley was exposed, this attitude leads almost inevitably to war crimes. It is summed up in the slogan "A few gooks more or less—what's the difference?" Those who put victory above everything else, who at most pay lip service to international law, who would cover up war crimes, who can see no difference between unavoidable killings of non-combatants and deliberately executing them to avoid inconvenience, who advocate methods of indiscriminate mass killing and destruction—these are on the way to adopting the attitude I mean. Those who see the connection between this attitude and the proneness to war crimes under conditions of strain, yet themselves adopt that attitude and encourage it in others, fail in their internal responsibility and I believe can be said to bear a share—collectively a not inconsiderable share—of the responsibility for the massacre at My Lai.

R. S. DOWNIE

Responsibility and Social Roles

Discussions of the large-scale crimes or tragedies of human history characteristically produce two lines of argument: that for any crime there must be some individual or individuals who can be blamed, and, to the contrary, that it is unfair or unrealistic to blame individuals for it is really 'the system' which is to be blamed. Both lines of argument have been followed in the discussions which centered on the court-martial of Lieutenant Calley, and comparable discussions can be found arising out of the trial of any alleged war criminal. Let us call the first approach "individualism" and the second "collectivism."[1] These approaches can be made to seem independently plausible, though mutually contradictory, and hence, quite apart from the obscurity in the facts of the My Lai incident, the theoretical issues in the debate have not always emerged clearly. While a philosopher has no special competence in sifting facts, he at least can hope to clarify

[1] I have dealt in much more detail with the problems of individualism and collectivism in *Government Action and Morality* (London: Macmillan, 1964) and *Roles and Values* (London: Methuen, 1971; New York, Barnes and Noble).

the theoretical issues. The aim of this paper will therefore be to deal at some length and in general terms with the natural dialectic of the individualist and the collectivist approaches to the ascription of moral responsibility, and then to apply this theoretical apparatus to the specific case of Lieutenant Calley.

The Individualist Approach

The individualist might begin by arguing as follows. First of all, he will assert that actions performed by individual persons, and only such actions, are appropriate subjects for moral predicates of the kind that are used in ascribing blame or moral responsibility. He will then point out that the actions of collectives are not the actions of individuals and conclude that the actions of collectives are therefore not appropriate targets for moral judgments. Because this argument is logically valid, we must examine the truth of the premises.

The major premise is that it is legitimate to pass moral judgments on an action if, and only if, it is performed by an individual. Is this the view that it is a *sufficient* condition of an action's being the appropriate target of a moral judgment that it be performed by an individual person? This is a strong thesis the investigation of which produces many arguments of relevance to moral philosophy. But as far as our present interest in the premise is concerned we need attribute to the individualist only the weaker thesis that it is a *necessary* condition of an action's being suitable for moral judgment that it be performed by an individual. It is not yet clear, however, whether when the individualist says that it is suitable, appropriate, or legitimate to make moral judgments only about the actions of individuals, he means that it is *logically* suitable, or whether he means that it is *morally* suitable. The answer to this question depends on the nature of the arguments used to defend the premise.

One argument might be what is often called the "'ought' implies 'can' argument": that if there is anything a person categorically or morally ought to do then he must unconditionally be able to do it, although he may or may not in fact do it. This argument can be criticised from various point of view, but from our present point of view its defect is that by itself it does not succeed in establishing the required necessary connection between individual action and moral predicates. It would surely be possible for a *group* to have this freedom to act otherwise. Only if we analyse freedom (as Kant perhaps does) in such a way that the necessary conditions for possessing it can be found only in an individual person does the argument succeed, and in that case it has succeeded at the price of begging the question. To say this is not, of course, to reject the " 'ought' implies 'can' arguments" as such, nor even to reject the Kantian analysis of freedom, but simply to reject the argument as an independent basis for establishing the major premise of the individualist's position.

A second line might be called the "pragmatist's argument": that it is socially desirable to connect moral responsibility with individual action because the establishment of such a connexion provides a social atmosphere friendly towards law and order. There is clearly a close connexion between moral responsibility and legal responsibility, particularly criminal responsibility, and it is therefore useful and desirable to assume that when it is legitimate to think of blame for some action it is necessary to look for particular individuals on whom to pin the blame. The trouble with the pragmatist's argument here, however, is that, like many other pragmatic arguments, it does not bear on the question of the *truth* of the individualist's major premise. It establishes only (what is no doubt plausible as far as it goes) that it makes for stability in society to assume that behind any moral or criminal failing there is always some one individual or individuals on whom the blame can be pinned. No doubt it would also be desirable as a means of social control if we all assented to the proposition "God exists," but the usefulness of the belief would not establish its truth.

It is in fact probable that there is no argument which would independently establish the individualist's major premise. Any argument which seems plausible will turn out to be presupposing the premise. We are therefore forced to conclude that we have in the major premise a fundamental assumption of the moral point of view. In other words, if blame is logically to count as *moral* blame the actions concerned logically must have been performed by individual persons. It might be objected at this point that whereas what I say may be true of certain moral points of view, it is not true of everything that might be called a 'moral point of view.' But is this really so? Certainly, there may be sets of beliefs which do not make this assumption, and those beliefs may have many resemblances to what we might call moral beliefs. It is arguable, however, that what has come to be known as 'morality' in civilised nations (say, those which signed the U.N. Declaration of Rights) is necessarily connected with the free decisions of individuals. At the very least, we can say that it is in terms of this morality that the debate over Lieutenant Calley is conducted. The position then is that it is *logically* appropriate to look for individuals on whom to pin moral blame, although this logical truth may be based on a foundation of the contingent historical development of a set of assumptions about the individual and his actions. Let us now move to the minor premise in the individualist's argument.

The minor premise is that the actions of collectives are not the actions of individuals. The defence of this premise might be that it is simply a matter of definition that if collectives are acting then we cannot also say that individuals are acting. But this conclusion may be too hasty. After all, if a voice at the other end of the telephone says, "This is Allied Metals Incorporated speaking" we do not imagine that the voice proceeds from anything other than another individual person (unless, of course, a telephone answering machine!). This suggests that the disjunction implied in the individualist's minor premise is invalid, that it does not follow from the fact that a collective is acting that some individual or individuals are not *also* acting. Why then do we speak at all of "collective" action? The answer might be that it is convenient to do so—that a "collective" is simply an abbreviation to refer to the sum total of the individual actions of some group. For example, the collective term "government" might be said simply to refer in abbreviation to the *members* of the government, and the term "U.S. Army" to refer to the individual soldiers who at any given time make up the U.S. Army. If this approach is accepted the dispute between the individualist and the collectivist disappears because both can accept the major premise that moral predicates are properly applied only to individual persons, and the apparent disagreement between them over the minor premise can be shown to be based on a failure to realise that the term "collective" is just an abbreviation or fiction which enables us to discuss conveniently the actions of certain groups of individuals.

This argument is plausible over a certain area. For example, if a group of students are in high spirits one afternoon and decide to paint a beard on the statue of the college's leading benefactress, then the college authorities may rightly decide that each of the students in the group is individually morally culpable and act accordingly. In this case the moral responsibility of the collective reduces without remainder to the individual responsibilities of the students who make up the collective. But what of the college authorities? Do they constitute a collective whose responsibilities can be reduced to the individual responsibilities of the members? This does not seem to be the case. College authorities can introduce ordinances which may be binding long after the actual professors who introduced the rules have retired—just as the British Government regarded itself as bound in 1914 by a Treaty made with Belgium in 1839. Again, the purposes of the college authorities in acquiring land in order to erect a new building are not the purposes of Professor X and Professor Y who happen to be concerned at a given moment in history with that side to the college policy. The general point is that, to provide an adequate description of the actions, purposes, and responsibilities of a certain range of collectives, such as governments, armies, colleges, incorporated business firms, etc., we must make use of concepts which logically cannot be analyzed in individualistic terms. For example, we require concepts such as "constitution" or "contract" or "authorisation" which cannot be analysed into what Professor X or Y happen to want to do.

It does not follow from these criticisms that we must abandon entirely the individualist's approach to collective responsibility and give to the collective some metaphysical existence. Some philosophers in the past have rightly seen that the actions, purposes, and responsibilities of certain collectives, such as governments or states, cannot be exhaustively analysed in terms of the actions, purposes, and responsibilities of private individual persons, and they have concluded that collectives such as states are superentities with their own mystical form of existence. Such beliefs are bad (and dangerous) metaphysics. The claim that individual persons and only such are morally responsible is a truth of the metaphysics of morality, but the claim that collective actions are not exhaustively analysable into the actions of individual persons is a truth of the philosophy of law. We require a theory which allows us to incorporated both truths without committing us to the existence of mystical entities.

The stumbling block in the analysis has been the assumption that actions by individual persons in a private capacity and by collectives in a public or official capacity exhaust the possibilities. This disjunction must be rejected because an individual person can act in a public or official capacity. Helpful here is the concept of a social role, understood for this purpose as being a set of rights and duties to be analysed in terms of institutional concepts. An individual person is able to act not only in a private capacity but in that of a social role, and this concept, understood institutionally, enables us to do justice to the valid points in the collectivist's case, for it is logically unanalysable in purely individualistic terms. Yet the concept of social role, so understood, also enables us to do justice to the individualist's insistence that moral responsibility must remain with the individual person, for we can say that, in so far as an individual consents to act in a role, he or she thereby becomes morally responsible for the actions which are done in its name. In accepting the role he adds to his share of rights and duties those which go with the role; if he feels unable to accept the rights and duties of the role he can refuse to accept the role. Here, then, we have the beginnings of a theory which will enable us to agree with the individualist that moral responsibility belongs ultimately to individuals, while also agreeing with the collectivist that there is much more to collective action than can be explained in terms of individuals acting in a purely private capacity. We can call this first dimension of collective responsibility 'the morality of role-acceptance.' The problems in this dimension are those of when an individual should accept a given role, when he should resign, or (if resignation is for some reason inappropriate or impossible) when he should refuse to carry out the apparent duties of the role.

When collectives act individuals act, but those individuals act in roles whose capacities are defined by the nature of the collective. To put it another way, we can say that the individuals are *authorised* by their collectives to act in certain ways, depending on the function of the collective. Or the matter could be put in yet another way if we said that an individual could be made the representative of the collective. Now the terms of the authorisation will vary a great deal. For example, at one extreme a junior clerk may be authorised to stamp certain documents if and only if certain conditions hold; at the other extreme a teacher may be authorised to teach a certain historical period and given no directive as to how he must do this. In the latter case there is clearly room for a new dimension of moral responsibility which we can call the "morality of role-enactment." Indeed, even in the former case there is some, although very little, scope for variation in role-enactment. For example, questions of speed, neatness, and courtesy might be raised over the role-enacting of the clerk; but the enactment of the rights and duties which constitute roles of the latter type characteristically leaves much greater scope for the initiative of individuals, and the greater the scope the more room there is for moral judgments about the enactment of the roles.

The third dimension to the morality of collective action we can call the morality of the role as such. We can and often do pass moral judgments about certain roles or offices on the grounds that they are likely to lead to good or bad actions, irrespective of who occupies them. For example, it might be said that the role of secret policeman is evil in that if it is operated it will lead to evil action no matter who the secret policeman is. If a society is characterised in total abstraction from its members, this concept generally suggests the morality of the system of roles. This point is illustrated by Gandhi who, when speaking of the British government in India, said ". . . an Englishman in office is different from an Englishman outside . . . Here in India you belong to a system which is vile beyond description. It is possible, therefore, for me to condemn the system in the strongest terms, without considering you to be bad and without imputing bad motives to every Englishman."[2] This is a characterisation of a system of roles conceived in abstraction from its operators.

It should be noted that the justification for using the language of moral, as distinct from natural, good and evil in speaking of a

[2] Quoted by C. F. Andrews, *Mahatma Gandhi's Ideas,* p. 241 (London: Allen and Unwin, 1929).

system of roles does not lie merely in the fact that the roles, if operated, will lead to morally good or evil actions. The roles themselves are connected with human decision in a manner such as will justify their assessment in moral language. The connection lies in the fact that society is a human artefact; it has been built up as a result of innumerable human judgments, decisions and acceptances in the past. Of course, not all the judgments and decisions which have led to the creation and development of our social institutions are to be assessed in moral language: many will simply be the result of the mistakes or happy chances which inevitably follow from limited human knowledge, and honest mistake of fact is hardly to be assessed in moral terms. Moreover, some of our institutions can less properly be said to have been built up by judgment and decision than to have grown up by custom: we did not so much create them as find ourselves in possession of them. Nevertheless, among the judgments and decisions which have created our social institutions are some to which both praise and blame can be attached, and those institutions which have grown up by custom are at least accepted by us; even if we did not make them we do consent to their presence. Our institutions, then, are images of ourselves as moral creatures. It is society, rather than the individuals now acting in their roles, which is responsible in this sense, because the individual does not necessarily choose the actions to which his role commits him. This is a dimension of collective *moral* responsibility because there remains a connection, although an oblique one, between the actions resulting from the nature of the role and individual human decision. But it is only one dimension of collective moral responsibility, since we clearly must make room for the first and second dimensions as well.

We have, then, three dimensions of moral responsibility in collective action—the morality of the role, the role-enactment, and the role-acceptance—and the complex nature of judgments of collective responsibility is due to the fact that all three dimensions may be relevant. Let us consider in more detail (and in that order) the interplay of these dimensions.

The Collectivist Approach

One way in which an individual may try to avoid blame is to shift the responsibility on to the institution or social role in which he is acting. For example, a policeman may say, *"I'm afraid* I must arrest you," thus disclaiming personal responsibility for the action and imputing responsibility to his social role. If such disclaimers are accepted, our further assessments are of the morality of the relevant role or system of roles. We say, for instance, "The whole system is rotten," and thus express our moral condemnation of a social system, while at the same time indicating a sense of bafflement over the precise location of responsibility for the creation of this state of affairs. In such a way, as has already been observed, Gandhi condemned the British Government in India without imputing bad motives to every government official. Similarly, cases of the deliberate burning of crops for economic reasons have the characteristics of moral evil, but the blame does not generally rest with a single person or group; the actions are more often a consequence of the economic structure of society. It is in such contexts, when a person feels he is not personally to blame for an action he has performed, that he is likely to say, "I was only doing my duty," or, "It is part of my job," or "I am not responsible for this decision." By means of such expressions we attempt to shift the blame on to the nature of the role, or (it may be) we modestly disclaim personal merit for an action.

Nevertheless, a person cannot always escape responsibility by saying, "I was only doing my job," because he may be told, "Yes, but you needn't have been so officious," or (by way of praise), "But you went to a lot of trouble over it." Such evaluations are concerned not with the morality of the role, but with the morality of role-enactment. There are a number of concepts such as devotion, tact, frankness, clumsiness, time-serving, and "working to role" which bear on the morality of role-eactment, and they all witness to the fact that, even though actions are performed by individual agents in a role, the personal qualities and ideals of the agent will affect the concrete action in varying degrees and ways.

Even if it is admitted that a person enacted a role as well as he could, he may still be open to the charge that he should never have accepted the role in the first place. Indeed, it is notorious that some criminals enact their corrupt roles with the highest personal qualities of courage, resolution, and loyalty. There is therefore the possibility of a dislocation between our assessments of the morality of the role and of the role-enactment. This throws into prominence a third aspect of moral responsibility, for the clarification of which another dimension is necessary. The third dimension is that of role-acceptance.

The morality of role-acceptance is involved when we say, "You ought to have gone into the implications of your job," or "You ought to have realised what would be expected of you," or "You ought to resign rather than be a party to such practices," or "You agreed to be responsible for him—for that—to him." In terms of the third dimension, then, a person is held to be responsible not just in the sense that it is he who carries out the actions with a certain quality, but responsible as he would be supposing he had also created the role. In so far as he did not bother to envisage the kinds of actions which would be expected of him, he is morally blameworthy, but in any case he can resign or refuse to obey orders.

The power of the third dimension to elucidate moral concepts is not likely to be disputed, but objection is likely to be leveled at the assumption that what is here described is merely an abstraction from a total moral situation. The basis of the objection is that what we have called the morality of role-acceptance is more familiar as the doctrine of the autonomy of the will, and this doctrine is fundamental to the individualistic approach to ethics. Hence, one must provide some reasons for the assumption that in discussing the morality of role-acceptance one discusses merely a single aspect of collective moral responsibility, and not a conception that gives the whole truth about the subject.

The main reason is that a person is not an isolated unit in society, and if he withdraws from one role he may bring hardship on the other persons with whom he is involved. Thus, the man who resigns from his job may involve his family in financial hardship and so fail at least partially in his role as a father. Sometimes, of course, withdrawal may be justified whatever the cost, and indeed sometimes suicide may be the only morally right course. But the decision whether or not to resign is rarely based on straightforward issues, and such may be the morality of the system of roles in which a person is caught up that moral evil will result whatever he does.

It is worth noting that a common device adopted to escape the tensions produced by this situation involves a conscious or implicit restriction of the areas of life to which moral considerations are allowed to apply. Thus, moral considerations are sometimes said to be applicable only to private or personal matters while public or official life remains outside their jurisdiction. The ethics of this attitude are expressed in such significant tautologies as, "War is war," or "Orders are orders." But where a person honestly faces up to conflicts between his roles, or between his roles and his own moral beliefs, we have situations which require for their adequate analysis the first as well as the third dimension of assessment.

Finally, the analysis of other situations may require the second as well as the third dimension. A person may hate his role and all its implications but still feel obliged to remain in it because, by opting out, he will leave the role open for someone without even his scruples. There are various ways in which a role can be enacted, and a person can bring to his actions a quality which may either mitigate or exacerbate its evil effects. Thus there may be morally good reasons for remaining in a morally bad role.

MORAL RESPONSIBILITY FOR MY LAI

We are now in a position to put the case of Lieutenant Calley into the conceptual structure which has been developed in general terms. Naturally, we shall not argue the rights and wrongs of the particular case because to do so in a convincing way requires a detailed review of the facts of the case, and detailed reviews of facts lie outside the legitimate province of philosophers. It is sufficient for philosophical purposes if we can state the general principles which might be involved in actual assessment of the case. The relevant dimensions of assessment have so far uncovered are the morality of the role (in this case that of the army officer), the morality of the role-enactment (how efficiently, blindly, humanely, intelligently, etc.) he carried out his orders, and the morality of the role-acceptance—how far he freely chose to act in the role or how far he was drafted.

As far as the first dimension is concerned, it might be argued that very little can be said because the role of army officer and the rights and duties which constitute it are well-known, and there is no reason to hold that there was anything reprehensible about it in this case. If moral judgments are to be made hostile to the role of army officer they must be made (it can be argued) from the point of view of pacifism. The reason is that an army consists of a tightly-locking system of a kind such that it is impossible to criticise one element in it without attacking the whole conception of a military organization as immoral. While there no doubt may be a good deal to be said for this anti-military position it might be thought to be misleading to say it in the context of a specific alleged atrocity.

The pacifist can reply, of course, that it is precisely in the context of a specific atrocity that the force of his general case can be understood. Just as it is when we see actual instances of the deliberate destruction of crops for economic reasons that we might understand the claims of those who assert that the whole economic system is rotten, so it is in the context of an actual atrocity that we can understand the position of someone who maintains that having any military organization is wrong because it cannot but lead to incidents of this sort. Indeed, this kind of argument could be used in defence of Lieutenant Calley. Thus, it might be contended that it is unfair to single out certain individuals and to make scapegoats of them, since the types of action for which they are being blamed are not only common among other soldiers but are indeed the inevitable outcome of the types of situation in which soldiers cannot but find themselves placed. A full statement of this position requires the extension of the argument beyond the condemnation of the military system to a more general indictment of a whole social system, and we shall shortly consider this kind of extended moral judgment on a whole social system. But the argument which criticises the system of military roles as such has probably been stated sufficiently fully to make clear how it tends to shift moral censure from the individual to the system.

It is possible, however, to make out a case for blaming the individual *as well as* blaming the system of roles in the restricted military sense of system. To do this is to bring into focus another dimension of moral assessment—that of the morality of role-acceptance. It can be argued that, after all, an individual is free and not obliged to accept the rights and duties of a particular role, and in many cases this is true. If a man does not approve of a certain business concern there is no need for him to agree to accept a job with it, or, if he has accepted a job and does not like the way it has turned out, he can resign. As we have seen, this simple position is barely tenable even in the context of ordinary business concerns, but, obviously, when the organization is an army the simple position omits two essentially relevant factors. The first is that it may not be true to say that the soldier accepted the job of his own free will, for he may have been very reluctantly drafted. The second is that it is quite misleading to speak of 'resignation' in a military context. The organization of a military system is very strict and authoritarian and cannot allow a place for the normal escape routes from unpleasant duties. What in a civilian context is "resignation" must in a military context become "refusal to obey orders," and this is the cardinal sin of the soldier. The point is not that it would never be right to do this but that it is a much more serious step than resignation in a civilian context. What we have in general characterised as "the morality of role-acceptance" becomes, then, in a military context, "the morality of disobeying orders," and as such it is clearly a large and thorny topic on its own.

But some would say that the case of Calley is most profitably and relevantly discussed in the dimension of the morality of role-enactment. In other words, we can discuss it so as to bring out its striking features without raising the general questions of the morality of there being military organizations, the morality of the military roles as such, or the morality of disobeying orders in a military context. We can do this, it might be said, because the interest of the Calley case centres on the way he carried out his orders, which in our conceptual scheme is the morality of the role-enactment.

In discussing this we are required to bear in mind a number of factors. For example, we would be required to know what exactly Calley's orders were, for if he did exactly what he was himself ordered to do then this would certainly widen the area of responsibility. Again, if his orders were ambiguous or in some way required interpretation, he would need to decide whether the interpretation which he put on them was such as might have been put on them by a reasonable officer in the circumstances. Clearly, part of the debate was in fact conducted along these lines.

There is, however, a radical objection to conducting the debate along lines such as these, and the investigation of this objection will open up once again the broad issues which we touched on in discussing the morality of the role as such. The radical objection can take several connected forms. One form is to say that it is unrealistic to apply categories such as 'reasonableness' in cases of extreme fear or tension. The processes of the criminal law and all the categories which go with it, it might be said, are intended to apply in basically law-abiding communities. In situations of extreme fear, however, it is quite unrealistic to expect soldiers to behave as they would in their hometown, and the deterrents of the criminal law are in any case quite useless for affecting their conduct. Another form of the objection (which can be used in conjunction with the first) is that it is unfair to single out certain individuals and to make scape-goats of them, because the types of action for which they are being blamed are common among soldiers, or indeed are necessary for the survival of the soldiers in the situations in which they have been placed by others. A third form of the radical objection—again consistent with and often used in conjunction with the first two—is that the values of the people passing judgment on soldiers like Calley are such that had they been placed in the solders' situations they would have found themselves acting in similar ways. Let us consider the consequences of accepting the general drift of objections of this type.

First of all, we should note that it does not necessarily exonerate Calley or his like. The fact that someone else is to blame for putting a person in a difficult situation does not by itself excuse evil conduct in the situation. At best it ought to mitigate penalties for bad conduct in the situation. Of course, if it can be established that extreme fear has so operated on a person that he no longer knows what he is doing, then this might excuse; but such defences are difficult to establish. It might be more realistic in cases such as that of Calley to regard the fear as creating a form of duress which would mitigate his blameworthiness although not entirely exonerate him.

Secondly, if we accept that the radical type of objection widens the area of moral blame, it might be said to bring into focus the part played by the U.S. government in all this, for clearly the U.S. army was in Vietnam as a result of government policy over a period of years. But even this does not take us far enough, for even if the policy-makers must take some moral blame for creating the general situation in which the army was obliged to do what it did, the policy-makers themselves are in some sense, however indirect, reflecting the aims of the majority of the U.S. public. Such conclusions follow from the existence of democratic systems of government.

We have then a sense in which moral blame can be meted out to "the system." The situation in which Calley and others in Vietnam found themselves was not exactly of their own creation, and it might well be that the best they could often hope to do was to choose the lesser of two evils in their conduct of the war. They would remain morally responsible for their actions in that they could always refuse to obey orders, or indeed refuse to be drafted, although these policies carried out by individuals raise complex moral problems of their own. They would also remain morally responsible for the way they carried out their orders—for the morality of their role-enactment—because even morally bad policies can have their evil effects mitigated by certain ways of putting them into practice. But we also have a sense in which it is legitimate to blame "the system." We can do so in so far as we can see the policies of the army as being created by other individuals in their roles, and we can see these policies as attempts to follow the general wishes of the electorate.

We have not, however, exhausted the nature of the shame which many Americans felt at the actions of Calley and others. So far we have depicted Calley as the delegated agent of the army and indirectly of the U.S. electorate. This enabled us to isolate two dimensions of the morality of the situation—that of the role-acceptance and the role-enactment—which apply to the agent, and a third dimension—that of the role as such—which applies to the authorising or delegating principal, the Pentagon and indirectly the U.S. electorate. Still there was another sense in which Calley was felt to be a representative of the U.S. people. In this sense we might say he was a *typical* American boy, he accepted and shared values which would be widely shared by other ordinary Americans. His conduct at My Lai, however, seemed to cast doubt on these values in two respects. First of all, if someone claiming to accept these values can nevertheless behave in a murderous way in certain situations, then there is an implication to be drawn that the values are simply a veneer. Secondly, and more radically, if these values have been pursued consistently and such dreadful situations have resulted, then the implication seems to be that there is something fundamentally wrong with the values themselves. It is the suspicion that the last point may be valid which has led not only to deep American interest in the case but also to widespread world interest.

DAVID COOPER

Responsibility and the "System"

Unquestionably, Lt. Calley was a victim of a system which brings home the horrors of war.

—R. Askew, Governor of Florida

The boy is a product of the system.

—George Lattimer,
Calley's civilian defense lawyer

[*Lt. Calley*] *is a product of our system . . . not only a product but also a victim of our system.*

—Senator Lawton Chiles

WHEN THE "SYSTEM" IS RESPONSIBLE

THESE COMMENTS ON LT. CALLEY, made shortly after his conviction for the premeditated murder of an unspecified number of civilians at My Lai, are representative of a common public attitude at the time. According to one poll, eighty percent of Americans opposed the verdict or sentence. The majority of those opposed did so on the grounds that it was not Calley who was primarily responsible, but rather some "system" which was the main bearer of guilt, even though few people made clear just what this "system" was supposed to comprise.

Accusations against groups, collectives, or systems did not begin with the My Lai trials. In 1967 the so-called International War Crimes Tribunal, set up through the efforts of Bertrand Russell, put "on trial" not individual American soldiers, but America itself. Indeed "the Tribunal unanimously declared the United States guilty of the crime of genocide,"[1] and Jean-Paul Sartre, in

[1] El Kaim-Sartre, A summary of the evidence and judgments of the International War Crimes Tribunal, in Jean-Paul Sartre, *On Genocide* (Boston: Beacon, 1968).

a speech before the Tribunal, bluntly declared that *America is guilty.*[2]

Our aim, then, is to understand and assess claims to the effect that a "system," whatever it might include, is morally responsible for the My Lai massacres and for atrocities of a similar kind. We are not going to discuss the individual guilt of Lt. Calley or any other single soldier, for whether or not a "system" bears some responsibility for the atrocities is not strictly relevant to the issue of Calley's guilt. That he was part of, or a "product" of, a "system" which bears responsibility might be reason for sympathizing with him or for mitigating his sentence, but it certainly does not show that he is innocent of the charges brought against him. Those who referred to him as a "scapegoat" are simply confusing innocence with grounds for sympathy. But rather than involve ourselves in these questions of Calley's individual guilt, we shall only discuss responsibility for wider aspects of American military practice—such as the bombing of villages—and only in so far as this might bear upon the question of responsibility for My Lai and similar atrocities committed by ground troops against unarmed civilians. There are those who refuse to see any moral distinction between My Lai and the bombings. "What is the difference between Calley and a bomber pilot?" is a popular question. The answer is that there may well be several moral differences, and if there are relevant differences, it will only be confusing to lump together the various types of alleged war crimes.

When a person accuses a group or system, he sometimes is doing so simply as a shorthand way of accusing certain specific individuals who happen to belong to the group or system. A person who holds a football team responsible for damage done to a hotel during a victory celebration might mean no more than that certain specific players—the quarterback, left linebacker, etc.—are individually responsible. It is just simpler for him to talk of the football team, rather than mention each player separately. This is what accusations against a "system" in Vietnam sometimes seem to come to. One journalist, for example, having condemned the "system," then proceeds to explain that by this he means to condemn certain individuals, and he mentions Johnson,

[2] *Ibid.*, p. 83.

Nixon, Laird, Rostow, Rusk, and Kissinger.[3] In this sense, then, to say "The system is responsible" is equivalent to saying "Individuals A, B, . . . , N are responsible." No doubt it is crucial to decide which individuals are to be blamed for war crimes in Vietnam, from Lt. Calley to men in the highest positions; but we are not concerned here with the responsibility of a "system" in the sense in which this is equivalent to the responsibilities of certain individuals. We are concerned, rather, with the sort of case where a person might say "I don't necessarily blame any particular individual; it's the system as a whole that is to blame." These are cases where the statement that "The system is responsible" is not equivalent to the statement that "Individuals A, B, . . . , N are responsible." Karl Marx, for example, makes it clear that he holds the capitalist system and class responsible for much of the misery in industrial society:

> Inasmuch as I consider the development of the economic structure of society to be a natural process, I should be the last to hold the individual responsible for conditions whose creature he is.[4]

For Marx, then, condemning the capitalist system is by no means equivalent to condemning each, or indeed any, individual capitalist. It is the "system," whose members are somehow tools, dupes, or products and creatures of it, that is to blame. This distinction sketched between two ways of ascribing responsibility to a group or system needs to be made more precise. Further we must ask if the type of ascription that concerns us really makes sense. How can a "system" be morally responsible without any individual having to be responsible? This will be the question for the next section. On the assumption that systems can be responsible, we shall ask in the last section if there is some "system" in Vietnam to be blamed for the My Lais of the war.

DISTRIBUTIVE AND NON-DISTRIBUTIVE RESPONSIBILITY

It seems, then, that ascribing responsibility to groups or systems, where this is not equivalent to holding individuals responsible, is an intelligible practice with a rationale behind it. But before dis-

[3] Nicholas Von Hoffman, *The Miami Herald,* 30 March 1971.
[4] Karl Marx, *Capital* (Everyman, 1964), p. 864.

cussing the conditions under which such ascription is justified, let us first consider a few semi-formal terms. We shall define a group as any collection of people whose actions are up for collective assessment. In this wide sense, a family, a club, or a regiment could all be groups. Where a group is held responsible, but only as an abbreviatory device for holding individual members responsible, we shall say that the responsibility is *collective and distributive*. "Group responsibility so conceived," says Professor Feinberg, "is simply the sum of all individual responsibilities."[5] Responsibility here is distributed, without remainder, over various members of the group. Where, as in the case of Marx's indictment of capitalism, the responsibility of the group is not taken as equivalent to that of individuals, we shall say that it is *collective and non-distributive.*

Collective, non-distributive responsibility of a group can be related in three possible ways to individual responsibilities. First, there is the case where *no* member of the group is held individually responsible, as, for example, in Marx's indictment quoted above. Second, there is the case—probably the most common—where, although certain individuals are held responsible in some degree, the responsibility of the group is nevertheless not exhausted by these individual responsibilities. For example, one might be willing to single out certain capitalists as bearing special responsibility for the ills of society, yet still feel that in condemning the system one is doing far more than condemning these few men. Finally, there is the tricky case where one does hold *each* member of a group individually responsible, yet still feels that the responsibility of the group is something more than the sum of all these individual responsibilities. The German philosopher Jaspers, discussing the crimes of Hitler's Germany, writes:

> Every German is made to share the blame for the crimes committed in the name of the Reich . . . inasmuch as we let such a regime rise among us.[6]

[5] Joel Feinberg, "Collective Responsibility," *Journal of Philosophy,* 1968, p. 683.

[6] Karl Jaspers, "Differentiation of German Guilt," in H. Morris (ed.) *Guilt and Shame* (Belmont: Wadsworth, 1971), p. 40.

Yet, he insists, to condemn Germany is more than to condemn each German for his active or passive toleration of the Nazis, for it is also "the world of German ideas," "German thought," and "our national tradition" that are to blame. We might treat this as a way of saying that there is a group—in this case a whole nation—bearing responsibility over and above all individual responsibilities.

Does ascription of responsibility, in any of these ways, make sense? Some have urged on general philosophical grounds, that it does not. It is the tenet of a philosophical principle, sometimes known as "Methodological Individualism," that everything that can be said about a group is somehow "reducible" to what can be said about individuals composing the group.[7] The tenet derives, perhaps, from the feeling that were this not so, we should have to postulate the existence of certain entities or *groups*, over and above and in some form of isolation from, individual human beings. And this, it is feared, is simply unintelligible. What, for instance, can a club be except for a number of people related in various ways? Applied to the case of responsibility, the tenet suggests that only the ascription of *distributive* collective responsibility to groups is intelligible. There is something to be said for the principle of Methodological Individualism, but it can be misapplied if it is used to rule out the possibility of non-distributive group responsibility.

Perhaps the best way to show that non-distributive responsibility is a sensible notion is to describe a case where it would seem plausible to ascribe just that type of responsibility to a group, then we may reflect upon what is involved in the ascription. Imagine a small frontier township in the nineteenth-century American West. For purposes of law and order the citizens form themselves into a vigilante committee. From the very beginning, however, the committee has not been concerned with administering proper justice, but with protecting the interests of its citizens against those of strangers and citizens of other nearby townships. It has become the common practice, in any dispute, to uphold the

[7] For a discussion of this principle, see Karl Popper, *The Open Society and Its Enemies* (London: Routledge and Kegan Paul, 1945).

"rights" of a local citizen, and to drive the stranger out of town. Suppose that, after some thirty years of this practice, a typically unjust decision is made against a wandering cowboy, who is then driven out of town. A newspaperman in a neighbouring town writes "Vigilante committee of X-ville is responsible for injustice against cowboy."

It seems that, given certain further conditions, what the newspaperman says may well be true, but that it would not be correct to regard the responsibility of the committee as equivalent to the individual responsibilities of members. First, it is clear that we may condemn the committee, for it is due to its organization and practice that the cowboy received rough treatment. Further, we may assume that this practice is by no means the general rule among townships in the area; X-ville has not reached the standards in the administration of justice reached by other towns. Second, however, it is not clear that any individual townsman in the committee can be condemned and blamed. Each is following the practice which has become universal in the township. Each, we may assume, would risk ostracization, or worse, for himself and his family if he tried to oppose the practice. Even if one or two citizens were especially enthusiastic in meting out unjust treatment to strangers, it is not obvious that responsibility for injustice is restricted to them; and even if we decided that each man is to blame for allowing the system to be perpetuated, it is unclear that this amounts to the condemnation we give of the system itself. The system we might reckon to be an *evil* one, but we would not necessarily say that any particular citizen is an evil, as opposed to a weak or convention-bound, man or woman. We might, speaking in Marx's way, describe the individuals as "creatures" of a system into which they were born.

There is a rationale behind such an ascription of non-distributive responsibility. For us to condemn an agent—whether a man or a group—it is necessary that the agent has fallen below some standard which we can reasonably expect should be met. But there is no *prima facie* reason for supposing that the standards applied to groups are the same as those applied to individuals. There is as little reason for supposing this as for supposing that what makes a casserole taste good is the same as what makes each ingredient in the casserole taste good. A casserole can taste good even if each individual ingredient, by itself, does not. In the case of the township, the point may be this: the vigilante system is certainly below standard, yet no individual has necessarily fallen below standards which can reasonably be expected of an individual under the circumstances. One cannot reasonably expect a man to sacrifice friendship, the welfare of his family, or even his home, by standing out against what has become the accepted and normal practice in his township. Feinberg writes:

> No individual person can be blamed for not being a hero or a saint . . . but a whole people can be blamed for not producing a hero when the times require it, especially when the failure can be charged to some discernible elements in the group's 'way of life' that militates against heroism.[8]

The people of X-ville are to be condemned for engaging in unjust practices, practices which militate against producing the sort of men who would have it in them to oppose a system of injustice. In a not unrelated example from the film *Shane,* we do not condemn the individual farmers who do not act against the thugs who have taken over their lands, for the farmer who opposes them, with Shane's help, is a *hero.* But, as Feinberg puts it, might we not condemn the people for not having produced heroes earlier, when the times required heroes?

It should be clear, from these examples, that in ascribing non-distributive responsibility, we are not committed to postulating the existence of strange, supra-individual entities. One might as well conclude that a casserole exists over and above its ingredients. The point is simply that different standards may be applied to the behaviour of individuals and to the behaviour of groups. Methodological Individualism is acceptable if it is simply claiming that groups do not exist apart from their members. The mistake creeps in if it is insisted that anything we can say about a group must be immediately applicable to members of it—if, for example, it is insisted that a group's lapsing below a standard means that some individuals must also have lapsed below standards expected of individuals.

We have already established two conditions for ascribing non-

[8] Feinberg, *op. cit.,* p. 687.

distributive responsibility: first, a group has fallen below some standard; and, second, it is not necessarily the case that any individual has fallen below some standard, or, at any rate, below the same standard we are applying to the group. There is a third important condition which is suggested by the last passage quoted from Feinberg. If we are to blame a group for actions performed by members of it, this must be in virtue of some practice, mores, rules, or "way of life" which characterizes the group. To be condemned, a group must be more than a random collection of individuals; it must be a collection of people between whom there are various ties and bonds, whose behaviour is partly governed by common rules, conventions, or mores. While a family or a regiment could be such a group, a collection of passengers at a railway station could not. A man who is a member of a group may well commit a condemnable act, but unless his performing it results in some degree from his acting according to the customs and practices of the group, there is no reason for condemning the group rather than him alone. Unless there is some degree of group solidarity, or group "way of life," surely any responsibility the group may have simply dissolves into the individual responsibilities of members.

This should be even clearer where the group could also be described as a system. For men to belong to a system, there must be regulated practices expected of them in virtue of their belonging to the system. To condemn a system for acts committed by a member, it is surely necessary that the acts issue, in some manner, from the regulated practices or customs of the system. Suppose, for example, that the only acts of injustice committed by members of the X-ville vigilante committee were committed by the strong group of doctors in the committee when their interests were at stake. In that case, we should not be entitled to condemn the vigilante system, for the responsible members are not acting according to the rules or practices of that system. If any group is to be held non-distributively responsible here, it would be "The Doctors" or "The Medical Profession," for it is not, if you like, *qua* members of the vigilante system that the doctors act in the condemnable manner.

In summary, then, it is rational to ascribe collective, non-distributive responsibility to a group or system, where 1) members of a group perform undesirable acts; 2) their performing these acts is partly explained by their acting in accordance with the "way of life" of the group (i.e. the rules, mores, customs, etc. of the group); 3) these characteristics of the group's "way of life" are below standards we might reasonably expect the group to meet; and 4) it is not necessarily the case that members of the group, in performing the acts, are falling below standards we can reasonably expect individuals to meet.

Before applying these considerations to the questions of atrocities in Vietnam, it is useful to glance at an historical case which bears some resemblance to the Vietnam issue. At the Nuremberg trials it was not only individual Germans who were accused, for the charter which set up the trials stipulated that "the tribunal may declare . . . that the group or organization . . . was a criminal organization."[9] As a result, the German cabinet, the Nazi party leadership, and the German military leadership were all accused of war crimes or of crimes against humanity. The question was not whether individuals belonging to these organizations were guilty—though some plainly were—but whether, in addition, one could regard the organizations themselves as guilty. The motivation behind the trials is not hard to find. As one commentator wrote in connection with the military leadership:

> There was a general, though ill-defined feeling that the root of all the troubles which Germany brought on Europe was to be found in something which was usually called German militarism or Prussian militarism.[10]

Both the verdicts and the conduct of the trial illustrate the importance of establishing the second of the four conditions mentioned above. The prosecution had to show that individual criminals were acting in accordance with the practices, rules, etc.—the "way of life"—of the organizations, and not simply as individuals. Both the cabinet and the military leadership were acquitted because this could not be shown, so the Tribunal decided. The cabinet, it was said, was a "mere aggregate of administrative

[9] Article 9 of the Charter of the International Military Tribunal, which was annexed to the Agreement of London 1945.

[10] P. Calvocoressi, *Nuremberg: The Facts, the Law, and the Consequences* (New York: Macmillan, 1948), p. 93.

officers," and, in the case of the military leadership, it was decided that "the collection of officers lacked the cohesion or common functions necessary to constitute a group in the sense in which the word 'group' was used in the charter."[11] Only in the case of the party leadership did the charge stick, for there it could be most plausibly argued that individuals were acting according to the mores, rules, and practices which bound them together into a genuine group.

As interesting as the verdicts are the words of the American prosecutor, Telford Taylor, in his closing speech against the military leadership, for they reflect exactly the need for establishing the condition in question:

> They are more than a group; they are a class, almost a caste. They are a course of thought and a way of life. . . . That is why the exposure and discrediting of this group is far more important than the fate of the uniformed individuals in the box, or of any other members of this group as individuals.[12]

It is only if some similar charge can be made against some group or system in Vietnam that we shall be justified in ascribing non-distributive responsibility for atrocities in that war.

RESPONSIBILITY AND THE "SYSTEM" IN VIETNAM

The only "system" to which it would seem at all plausible to ascribe responsibility for atrocities in Vietnam would be the military system. We may let this include not only soldiers in Vietnam, but those in and out of Vietnam who have some responsibility for training men and developing strategies for the war. We may also let it include those civilians who are in positions of authority in the conduct of the war.

For us to condemn this system it will not be enough, as already discussed, to show that men within that system commit atrocities. In addition, one must establish that the committing of the atrocities is to be partially explained by soldiers acting in accordance with sub-standard practices, rules, or conventions governing that system's "way of life" in Vietnam. Three alleged characteristics

[11] Calvocoressi, *op. cit.*, p. 98.

[12] Quoted in Calvocoressi, *op. cit.*, p. 171 and 174–175.

of the system might be regarded as the sub-standard ones we require: two are implausible candidates; the third is not.

Once we have settled the criteria for ascribing responsibility to the military system, only empirical research can establish whether or not that system meets with these criteria. Although we can make tentative suggestions as to its responsibility, in the light of what seem to be well-known and well-established facts, it must be remembered that there is much that is not known about the Vietnam situation, so that facts not yet available to us might force us to revise our picture of the situation.

Racism in the military system. It has been suggested that the aspect of the system which is partly responsible for atrocities committed against civilians is the *racism* which permeates the military. Although this charge expressed by Jean-Paul Sartre is not necessarily plausible, it does help to highlight certain points. According to Sartre, atrocities of the My Lai type are instances of the *genocidal* crimes that Americans commit in Vietnam. The crimes are genocidal, he says, because "the armed forces of the United States are killing Vietnamese in Vietnam for the simple reason that they are Vietnamese."[13] This genocidal intent, he contends, "is apparent . . . in the *racism* of American soldiers . . ."[14] Since, for him, the atrocities are genocidal acts encouraged by the system's racism, the system is partly responsible for them.

There is, in fact, no evidence to suggest that any American charged with committing an atrocity has done so *for the simple reason* that his victims were Vietnamese. None of those on trial for My Lai, for example, displayed any signs of racist hatred. Further, ARVN troops have also committed atrocities against civilians, and racism can hardly be the explanation in their case. But let us waive these points and assume, for the sake of argument, that some Americans who committed atrocities were racists. This assumption does not begin to show that we condemn the military system, for it would have to be shown, in addition, that any individual's racism is somehow encouraged by being part of that system. The evidence for this seems extremely scant. Army

[13] Calvocoressi, *op. cit.,* p. 58.
[14] *Ibid.,* p. 79.

authorities, it would seem, even have made determined attempts to improve soldiers' attitudes towards the Vietnamese people.

What of the famous "Mere Gook Rule," of which so much was heard during the trials? This is the alleged "rule" that the life of a Vietnamese is to be taken into little or no account. Certainly the "rule" is objectionable, and if it is encouraged by military policy it provides a ground for condemning that policy. Yet it is far from clear that the existence, or even prevalence, of the "rule" is enough to make a case of *racism* against the military. The mere occurrence of the word "gook" tells us nothing. Soldiers are rarely hesitant to apply unflattering epithets to both friend and foe—kraut, limey, frog, jock, etc. Although it may be true that Americans have scant respect for men of a different race in Vietnam, this attitude may also be simply a trivial result of the fact that the only local citizens happen to be of a different race. There is nothing to show that they are paid scant respect *because* they belong to a different race. It is arguable, certainly, that American attitudes towards Vietnamese are worse than is usual for troop attitudes towards foreign civilians, but there are several explanations of this which would be more convincing than one of brute racism. First, relations between civilians and troops of another country stationed in their country for the purposes of war are rarely good, and U.S. forces have been stationed in Vietnam for this purpose for a remarkably long time. Second, the soldiers live among civilians, many of whom then turn out to be active enemy supporters, and, at the same time, the enemy is remarkably difficult to distinguish from innocent civilians. This is not to justify any maltreatment of civilians, but it is hardly surprising that the hostile feelings towards the enemy should be transferred towards civilians who in looks, language, custom, and dress are often indistinguishable from that enemy. It would surely be these factors which play the main role in fostering objectionable attitudes towards Vietnamese civilians.

We see, then, that there is no reason to condemn the system for atrocities committed by racist soldiers, if there are any such acts. In so far as some objectionable attitude, encapsulated in the "Mere Gook Rule," can be charged against the system, there is no reason for describing this as a racist attitude. It is one thing to behave badly towards men *because* they belong to a certain race.

It is quite another thing to behave badly towards men who *happen to be* of a different race, but *because* of reasons that may have nothing to do with race.

Training in the military system. One defense of Calley was that army training methods for and in Vietnam were partly to blame for the behavior of himself and others at My Lai. Latimer insisted that Calley was "trained to kill . . . taught to kill." Along these lines, the following charge might be brought against the military: the methods of training for Vietnam, while they do not encourage the commission of atrocities, nevertheless produce unthinking killers who are only too prone, as a result, to commit atrocities.

It is worth noting two peculiarities in this charge as it was made by Calley's defense. First, the lawyers sometimes used the defense that Calley and his men were raw recruits, with insufficient training to cope with a situation like My Lai:

> They were an orphan unit. There was no esprit. There were fears and stark horror present in the unit on its first assault, and when raw troops are used, disaster is courted.[15]

It is surely impossible to reconcile the two pictures here: one of Calley and his men as unthinking, machine-like killers, moulded by irresistible training and indoctrination; the other of Calley and his men as raw, nervous recruits, liable to panic. Second, Calley's lawyers made no attempt to explain why, if training turns out killing automata, the majority of men in Calley's unit, as well as the vast majority of troops faced by similar situations, did not massacre civilians.

These points give the lie to the charge being considered. It might be that the training produces troops who are more trigger-happy than they should be, but it would be a nasty parody to describe Calley or Meadlo as merely "trigger-happy." The absurdity of the charge is demonstrated by the fact that so few behave as Calley did. It may be, of course, that training—by putting guns in men's hands, and by encouraging aggression to-

[15] George Latimer, in his closing speech for the defense, quoted in Richard Hammer, *The Court-martial of Lt. Calley* (New York: Coward, McCann, and Geoghegan, 1971), p. 337.

wards an enemy—does produce in some men attitudes which later contribute to the committing of atrocities. But to condemn the training system for these attitudes, it is necessary to show that it is worse off in this respect than any alternative training methods. No training which is designed to produce efficient soldiers can, I think, fail to run the risk that the occasional product will be a potential murderer. For that reason there is no basis for condemning the American system merely because it too runs that risk. Recall that it is necessary for one aspect of a system to be sub-standard before we can condemn the system in light of this aspect.

Sometimes, as noted, almost the reverse charge was made: that the training was too inefficient to teach troops how to deal with a situation like My Lai. For example, it might be said that insufficient instructions were given on the handling of prisoners, or civilians, and in the laws of warfare. "The only training that was given us as far as the treatment and handling of prisoners," said Captain Medina, "was basically the five S's—search, silence, safeguard, speed, and segregate."[16] And Calley, discussing the training he had received concerning the Geneva conventions, remarked that "nothing stands out in my mind what was covered in the classes."[17]

If training on how to deal with prisoners is as poor as Medina says, and instruction on the Geneva conventions as unmemorable as Calley says, the army is to be censured. But it is very difficult to see how these faults could be seen as responsible for the My Lai's. One does not require detailed training on how to handle prisoners to know that one does not massacre unarmed civilians who were not prisoners anyway. Nor is it any defense of murdering civilians to point out that the classes in which the rules of warfare were discussed were unmemorable. As Judge Kennedy at Fort Benning put it, the relevant point is whether "a man of ordinary sense and understanding" would see that it was unlawful to kill civilians in the My Lai manner. To hold the army responsible for atrocities on these grounds would be as absurd as holding the university authorities responsible for my setting fire to

[16] Quoted in Hammer, *op. cit.*, p. 302.
[17] Quoted in Hammer, *op. cit.*, p. 240.

the classroom building on the grounds that they never told me I should not.

It seems, then, that there is no good evidence to show that the Army training methods are a sub-standard aspect of the military system which could explain the committing of atrocities by troops, and so serve as a basis for condemning that system.

The Conduct of the War by the Military System. In his book comparing Nazi war crimes with various acts in Vietnam, Telford Taylor, the former prosecutor at Nuremberg, writes:

> The ultimate question of "guilt" in the trials of the Son My (My Lai) troops is how far what they did departed from general American military practice in Vietnam as they had witnessed it.[18]

He continues that, if the troops were not departing from general practice, then one cannot try them "without, in substance, putting American military practice in Vietnam on trial."

The point is this: while it is not part of U.S. military policy to murder civilians in the My Lai manner, it *is* military policy to commit other kinds of atrocities and criminal acts. The result is to create an atmosphere, an ethos, in which it is only too easy for "murderers" of the Calley type to feel that they are scarcely deviating from official, approved policy. Neil Sheehan, in one of a series of articles on the war and its crimes, suggests that Calley could have been defended "on the ground that, given the general atmosphere in which the war was being conducted and his interpretation of his orders that morning in My Lai, he may not have been capable of a moral choice."[19] Though this defense may be too strong, it does make the point that Calley's behaviour may be partly explained by an atmosphere in which atrocities were taken for granted, an atmosphere encouraged, perhaps created, by criminal military strategies. It is not difficult to cite strategies which, assuming their existence, are alleged to be criminal and immoral: free fire zones; the high body-count policy; bombing

[18] Telford Taylor, *Nuremberg and Vietnam: An American Tragedy* (New York: Quadrangle, 1970), p. 160.

[19] *Miami Herald,* 31 March 1971. Oddly enough, only one of Calley's lawyers, Capt. Raby, took this line, but he was continually thwarted by the lines taken by the other lawyers.

of villages of minimal military importance; the use of men as human mine-sweepers; deportation of civilians into appalling concentration camps; the use of frightful weapons.

If these are widespread practices, it is not difficult to imagine their effects upon troops who live with them and witness them. As one helicopter pilot said:

> It used to bother me killing people 50 feet below me. . . . But after a while you get used to it. Now it doesn't bother me at all.[20]

And four veterans, writing to the *San Francisco Chronicle,* sympathized with the My Lai killers on the grounds that their attitudes were "indicative of troop attitudes that the army has allowed to develop and, alas, in many cases to prevail."[21] Nor, one suspects, is the state of mind reflected in the words of the following marching song so very rare:

> Bomb the schools and churches,
> Bomb the rice fields too,
> Show the children in the courtyard
> What napalm can do.[22]

Assuming, then, that the conduct of the war is as black as some have portrayed it, and assuming the influence I suggested upon troop attitudes, we may have arrived at what we were searching for: sub-standard aspects of the system partially responsible for the committing of atrocities by individuals within that system.

There are two possible lines of defense for the system here. One is to argue that the conduct of the war is not sub-standard—that one could not reasonably expect an army, faced by the sort of enemy and situation which exist in Vietnam, to conduct the war any other way. But, however sympathetic one might be with the American problem in Vietnam, it would be difficult to make this defense work. In the "Lieber Rules" of 1863, governing American military practice, otherwise criminal acts are justified if they are "indispensable for securing the ends of war."[23] Can it be said that Free Fire Zones, napalm, etc. are "indispensable" in the conduct

[20] *Miami Herald,* 21 March 1971.
[21] *San Francisco Chronicle,* 31 December 1968.
[22] Quoted in J. Schell, *The Military Half.* (New York: A. Knopf, 1968).
[23] Quoted in Taylor, *op. cit.,* p. 33.

of the war? There are few competent authorities today who would deny that the effect of such practices has been to alienate masses of the population and to hamper the war effort in a situation where civilian sympathy is an important weapon. Even if we admit that those responsible for the tactics adopted them in good faith, believing them to be indispensable, it must still be insisted that they adopted them hastily, without having conclusive grounds to think them indispensable. Nothing short of conclusive grounds could possibly justify conducting the war in such ways. Further, if we are concerned with the atmosphere created by such practices, it is important to note not just what the practices are but also how and in what spirit they are conducted. If there are to be Free Fire Zones, at least maximum precaution should be taken to ensure that no innocent civilians remain within them. If deportation is thought necessary, at least the conditions of the camps should be made as tolerable as possible. There is, unfortunately, little evidence that the military has attempted in these ways to mitigate the severity of their practices. Further, there are some practices—such as the high body-count "rule," or the use of humans as mine-sweepers—which could never be defended on grounds of military indispensability.

The second line of defense that might be taken on behalf of the "system," as opposed to individuals, would be this: the objectionable practices were adopted by certain specific generals and civilians in military authority. Once we have ascribed responsibility to them, there is no need to go on to speak of any further responsibility belonging to a system. I do not think this line of defense will work either. No doubt it is possible to specify certain individuals who bear a special responsibility for laying down the general lines of military practice in Vietnam. But I think it is clear that, having blamed these men, blame is not exhausted. Practice is made, or at least continued, by the myriad decisions of generals, colonels, majors, captains, lieutenants, or sergeants in the field or in the air. Soldiers come into Vietnam faced by a ready-made situation, with various policies and practices established as the norms. They proceed to act in accordance with those norms, hence perpetuating the system characterized by these norms. It seems we do have a genuine *system* here; an organization in which men do not choose and act as isolated individuals, but as men having roles to play, rules to follow, and a way of life in which they are constrained. The position is surely similar to, on a larger scale, our vigilante system of the last section.

It may be that certain individuals are to be singled out; it may even be that, as Jaspers claimed, each man who acts within the system bears some degree of responsibility. This responsibility, as so many veterans have discovered, may be a "burden of the individual who must get along with himself."[24] But that is not the end of responsibility, for these individuals act as parts of a system which they did not create, nor which was created by any few individuals. The Calleys of the war are no doubt morally and criminally responsible. But a system which has developed its own momentum—and which is not the creature of a few individuals, but rather whose creatures most individuals are—must bear its share of responsibility for the "unlovely circumstances" of the war, those circumstances which partially explain the existence of the Calleys.

[24] Jaspers, *op. cit.*, p. 51.

VIRGINIA HELD
Moral Responsibility and Collective Action

THERE CAN BE LITTLE doubt that something that can be impartially described as "a massacre," in which several hundred unarmed and unresisting persons including small children were indiscriminately shot and killed, occurred at the hamlet of My Lai 4 in the village of Son My in South Vietnam, on March 16, 1968. The massacre was carried out by men of Charlie Company, 1st Battalion, 20th Infantry, U.S. Army of the United States of America. The only person so far convicted of a crime in connection with the massacre is First Lieutenant William L. Calley. Not all the members of Charlie Company shot unarmed Vietnamese villagers that day, but to conclude that only Calley performed the action that we call "the massacre" is implausible. To conclude that the United States performed it is no less so. Who, or what, in such circumstances, can be thought to be "morally responsible"[1] for "the action"?

* The discussion of moral responsibility and collective action in the following article is based on my "Can A Random Collection of Individuals Be Morally Responsible?", *Journal of Philosophy,* 23 July, 1970.

[1] I shall not try in this article to discuss questions of *legal* responsibility

Normally, the members of an Armed Forces unit are the antithesis of a "random collection" of persons: their "command structure" rigidly defines relations of command and obedience between persons. Theoretically, any militarily significant action performed by a member of the unit should be in accord with a command from the unit's highest officer. Any action performed by the unit would then be a collective action for which the unit's commander would be responsible, on up, unit by inclusive unit, to the commander-in-chief of the armed forces. Obviously, degrees of responsibility for the actions of lesser units and their members must be considered, and responsibility must be considered for actions which are not thought to accord with the commands of the commander-in-chief even as they are transformed on down through the chain of command.

President Lyndon B. Johnson, then Commander-in-Chief of the Armed Forces of the United States, did not, as far as we know, issue commands which could be understood as justifying the claim: "the Commander-in-Chief commanded the massacre at My Lai." No one has seriously claimed that the massacre was necessary for the pursuit of any military objective, stated or unstated. The massacre, as far as we know, did occur. Who, then, is "responsible"?

There is a sense in which all persons can be thought to be morally responsible for all their actions if certain requirements, to be discussed later, are met. Thus, even if an individual soldier is directly ordered by his commanding officer to perform an action, *A*, in some sense *he*, rather than his commanding officer, is morally responsible for *A*. But a more helpful approach may often be to consider other points at which moral responsibility may be exercised: is the person responsible for being a member of the military unit in question, is he responsible for remaining a member, and thus subject, as a member, to its "command structure," and so on.

Whether Charlie Company's commanding officer, Captain Ernest L. Medina, did or did not order his men to kill everyone

---

for acts which may be illegal under the laws of war or other laws. On this subject see especially Telford Taylor, *Nuremberg and Vietnam: An American Tragedy* (New York: Quadrangle Books, 1970), and Richard Wasserstrom, "The Relevance of Nuremberg," *Philosophy & Public Affairs*, Fall, 1971 and "The Laws of War," *The Monist*, January, 1972.

in My Lai, and hence to shoot unarmed Vietnamese villagers, is a matter of dispute. Whether he could or could not have stopped the massacre is also a matter of dispute. But there can be little doubt that Charlie Company as a collectivity could have "stopped the massacre," at least in the sense of significantly reducing the carnage, by a collective effort to curb the outbreak of shooting in which unarmed adults and children were deliberately killed. The command structure of Charlie Company, however, did not seem to be commanding its men to stop the massacre. The men of Charlie Company were for the most part not aware of Army regulations forbidding the unnecessary shooting of unarmed civilians[2] as effective commands to which they were subject. Hence it is not implausible to think that in taking a collective action to stop the massacre, the men of Charlie Company would have been acting as an unorganized group of individual persons rather than as an armed forces unit acting under command. But *can an unorganized group of persons who happen to find themselves together by the accidents of history, "a random collection," we might say, be responsible for not taking a collective action?*

A random collection of persons may be distinguishable as a group in space and time—passengers on a train or pedestrians on a sidewalk, for instance—but it has no specifiable method for deciding to act. An organized group or collectivity, on the other hand, is distinguishable not only by the location and other characteristics that delimit its membership from other persons, but especially by its possession of a decision method for action. "Action" must here be understood in the wide sense of doing something or causing something to happen or not happen.

Before the question raised can be dealt with, a number of preliminary assumptions need to be considered. These assumptions

[2] The applicable United States Army Field Manual (1956 edition) stated that "the law of war places limits on the exercise of a belligerent's power and requires that belligerents refrain from employing any kind or degree of violence which is not actually necessary for military purposes and that they conduct hostilities with regard for the principles of humanity and chivalry." The "Rules of Engagement" issued by General William Westmoreland, the American commander, directed the troops to "use your fire power with care and discrimination, particularly in populated areas," and another directive called for the minimization of civilian casualties and the protection of villagers whether living in a Vietcong or Government controlled hamlet.

concern statements about collectivities and the possible moral responsibility of organized groups.

Some methodological individualists suppose that all statements about the actions of collectivities are in principle reducible to statements about the actions of actual human individuals.[3] One may assume that a refusal to endeavor such reductions is frequently justifiable on pragmatic grounds, at the very least. We often assert, without difficulty, such empirical statements as "The corporation manufactures *X*," or "State *W* provides higher welfare payments than state *Y*," or "The Democratic Party nominated *Z*." And we often decide, without difficulty, that such statements are true. To require a reduction of such statements to statements about individuals would often be tantamount to abandoning them altogether, and such abandonment would often, let us assume, be unacceptable.[4]

A separate argument is required for moral judgments. Even though we may be willing to allow that collectivities can act, the questions whether they can also be held responsible and whether they can be subject to moral judgment remain. Let us assume an affirmative answer to both.

Consider the requirements for moral responsibility at the level of an individual. To hold an individual responsible for an action requires that he be aware of the nature of the action, in the sense that he is not doing *A* in the belief that he is doing *B*, and it requires that the judgment "He could have done something else" be valid of the action he has performed.

To hold an individual *morally* responsible for an action requires that he be aware of what I shall call the *moral nature* of the action, which can be understood as either the moral import of

[3] See May Brodbeck, "Methodological Individualisms: Definition and Reduction," in Brodbeck, ed., *Readings in the Philosophy of the Social Sciences* (New York: Macmillan, 1968).

[4] In stating their frame of reference, Talcott Parsons, Edward A. Shils, and James Olds, representing many others in related fields, write, for instance, that "The *actor* is both a system of action and a point of reference. As a system of action the actor may be either an individual or a collectivity. . . . The *individual-collectivity* distinction is made on the basis of whether the actor in question is a personality system or a social system (a society or subsystem)." *Toward a General Theory of Action* (New York: Harper, 1962), p. 56.

the kind of action of which it is an instance or as the moral value of the consequences it may produce. These requirements are not meant to be equivalent to requirements for complete knowledge, either in the case of responsibility or in the case of moral responsibility. But they preclude holding a person responsible for the thoroughly unascertainable aspects of an action he performs. They require that he be aware of the kind of action he is performing, but not that he know everything about either its empirical or its moral aspects.

If, for example, an individual throws an explosive device into an open window, and as a result a child is killed, he may not have been able to foresee this particular consequence, but he could be said to have been aware of the moral nature of his action as an instance of actions that risk causing death. On the other hand, if an individual presses a doorbell and, by a mechanism of which he could have no knowledge, causes an explosion that kills a child, he could be said to be responsible for pressing the bell, but not for causing the child's death; he could not be said to be *morally* responsible even for pressing the doorbell, since he could not in this case have been aware of what turned out to be the moral nature of this particular act of doing so. He could be said to be morally responsible for the morally neutral act of pressing the bell—if this part of the total action is considered to have moral import—but not for the morally unfortunate action of pressing the bell and causing a child's death.

Again, if a person steals a car to go to the aid of a friend, he may be morally responsible for stealing the car if he knows that what he is doing is a case of stealing and not something else. And he may be morally responsible for trying to help a friend, if he is aware that that is what he is doing, even though he may not know whether even he considers the total action right or wrong and even though a more impartial judgment than his that the action *was* right or wrong, taking the relevant moral principles and consequences into account, was not ascertainable at the time of the action.

If these requirements for responsibility and moral responsibility can be met by individual persons, they can, I think, be met by collectivities. If the Democratic Party nominates Hubert Humphrey, it is not acting in the belief that it is nominating George

McGovern; if Dow Chemical Company manufactures napalm, it is aware that the product is not edible gelatin and aware of the kind of activity it is performing. And it may sometimes be as reasonable to assert that a collectivity could have done something else than nominate candidate *X* or manufacture product *Y* as to assert that an individual could have done something else than the action for which he is held responsible.

Let us assume, further, that we can make moral judgments about the actions of collectivities. The claims that "Alabama should provide higher welfare payments than it does," "Brown University ought to admit more black students," and "the U.S. should not bomb North Vietnam" appear to be meaningful moral claims, and we can assume that we are willing to attach the term *valid* to some moral judgments among competing claims. A *valid* moral judgment about the action of a collectivity requires, among other things, that the collectivity be morally responsible for the action in question.

The reductionist position (that ascriptions of responsibility to collectivities can always be reduced to ascriptions of responsibility to those individuals who compose the collectivity) is sometimes thought to have a special force in connection with holding collectivities morally responsible, but the same arguments apply against this position as against a reductionist program for descriptive assertions. Suppose someone is considering the justifiability of a personal economic boycott against Dow Chemical for manufacturing napalm or against Westinghouse for price-fixing. He may require judgments of the form "Corporation *Z* should not have done *A*," but he may have no need for further judgments concerning which corporation executives did what in connection with the action. He might happen to be interested in these separate judgments, and other persons, in Congress or in the Anti-Trust Division, might require them for their purposes, but the person considering an economic boycott against a corporation may sometimes justifiably assert that "Collectivity *C* should not have done *A*" without acceding to a reductionist demand.

Similarly, someone considering whether or not to join the Democratic Party or go to Brown University or immigrate to the United States may well make moral judgments about the actions of the Democratic Party or Brown University or the United States, but he may reject as impossible a reductionist program for such judgments. What Ernest Gellner said of reductionist translations of disposition statements applies as well to moral judgments: "Such translations would . . . be clumsy, long and vague, where the original statement about an institution or feature of the social scene was clear, brief and intelligible."[5]

And if we have no intention of accepting reductionist demands in practice, it is dishonest to concede them "in principle." I propose, then, an honest rejection. What should be conceded to the individualist, however, is that from the judgment "Collectivity *C* ought (ought not) to have done *A*," judgments of the form "Member *M* of *C* ought (ought not) to have done *A*" cannot be derived. From our attribution of an action, and moral responsibility, to a collectivity, it does not follow that the collectivity's members are morally responsible for the action of the collectivity.[6] It is quite possible that other judgments may be supplied indicating that the members are indeed morally responsible or that the members may be morally responsible for the quite different actions of having joined or of retaining membership in the collectivity in question, but judgments about the moral responsibility of its members are not logically derivable from judgments about the moral responsibility of a collectivity. "The Democratic Party is morally responsible for the nomination of Humphrey," and "The United States is morally responsible for sending its planes to bomb North Vietnam," may well be valid judgments, but from such judgments alone one cannot conclude that Democratic Party member *M* or U.S. political-system member *N* is morally responsible for the actions in question. Similarly, the judgment "C Company is

[5] Ernest Gellner, "Holism vs. Individualism," in Brodbeck, ed., *op. cit.*, p. 258.

[6] See Joel Feinberg, "Collective Responsibility," *Journal of Philosophy,* Nov. 7, 1968, pp. 674–688, for the beginning—but only the beginning—of such an argument. See also D. E. Cooper, "Collective Responsibility," *Philosophy,* July 1968, pp. 258–268, for a more developed consideration of it. A traditional rejection of what is called "the barbarous notion of collective or group responsibility" is given by H. D. Lewis in "The Non-Moral Notion of Collective Responsibility" in this volume.

morally responsible for military action *A*" may be a valid judgment, but from it alone it does not follow that soldier *S* of C Company is morally responsible for *A*.

These somewhat lengthy preliminaries out of the way, we can now turn to the question of whether a random collection of individuals can ever be held morally responsible. We have been dealing thus far with "requirements" for moral responsibility, rather than with the more precise—and in my view still premature for this context—notions of necessary and sufficient conditions, or good and conclusive reasons. I wish now to consider whether there are requirements that can ever be met for a random collection of individuals to be substituted for group *G* in a valid judgment that "*G* is morally responsible for *A* (or non-*A*)," or "*G* ought (ought not) to have done *A* (or non-*A*)."

A first question will be whether a random collection can act. We may consider statements such as "The audience left the theatre," or "The pedestrians blocked the sidewalk," examples of what might be thought to be actions taken by random collections. To the extent that action presupposes intention, there may of course be special problems. But even if we take the position that random collections can act, it is questionable whether they can be held morally responsible in normal circumstances. The action taken by a random collection and the collective action taken by an organized group must be distinguished: the former cannot be the outcome of a group decision method, but the latter can. And the requirements for moral responsibility appear to be such that they can be met by random collections only in special circumstances.

It is doubtful whether a random collection can often be "aware of the moral nature of its action" or that it "could have done something else" in ways that will satisfy the requirements for moral responsibility, even when the actions of the individual members of the random collection are ones for which those members are individually responsible. But if the action in question is one which could only be taken by the random collection as a group, can a random collection *ever* be morally responsible for the performance or nonperformance of a collective action?

If we say that, in special circumstances, a random collection can be aware of the moral nature of an act, we do not claim the existence of an inexplicable group awareness over and above the awareness of its individual members, only that we are sometimes entitled to say "Random collection *R* is aware that *p*," even though we cannot carry out a reductionist demand for statements about each individual member. We may know, for instance, that a collection of individuals is composed of normal persons and that the statement "The bystanders were aware that they were standing up" is true even though we may be unable to know which particular persons had this awareness, how many, or exactly who they were. Similarly, we could say that "the men were aware that if *S* shot *W* repeatedly, *W* would probably die," even though we may not know exactly which men were observing the shooting.

A parallel point can be made with regard to the claim that the random collection "could have done something else": in special circumstances, we may be entitled to say that it could. But what are these special circumstances?

I shall confine my discussion to the nonperformance of an action, and argue that when the action called for in a given situation is obvious to the reasonable person (which may require that the expected outcome of the action be clearly favorable), a random collection of individuals may be held responsible for not taking a collective action. When the action called for is not obvious to the reasonable person, however, a random collection may not be held responsible for failing to perform the action in question, but, in some cases, a random collection may be held responsible for not forming itself into an organized group capable of deciding which action to take.

Let us consider the following cases:

(1) Assume that there are seven apparently normal persons in a subway car; none is acquainted with any other; none are sitting together. The second smallest person of the seven rises, pushes the smallest to the floor, and, in full view and hearing of the remaining five, proceeds to beat and strangle his victim. If the remaining five persons do nothing for, say, ten minutes, at the end of which time interval the smallest person is dead, would we be able to make a valid judgment that "they ought to have subdued the strangler"? It is possible that no one of the five, acting alone, could have subdued him; it is extremely probable that action by

two or more of the group to subdue him would have succeeded, with no serious injury to themselves; the group was not so numerous that, if each member had acted, confusion would have resulted. In such a case we would, I think, hold the random collection morally responsible for its failure to act as a group.

There is, of course, a question concerning what we take "the action" to be: is it the act of subduing the strangler, or is it some or all of its "sub-acts," such as holding his arms and legs? Whether or not we can consider such a problem a merely verbal one,[7] which is doubtful, the problem would not seem to be inordinately greater for the action of a group than for the action of an individual. If an able-bodied adult were to look on for five minutes while a two-year-old child slashed an infant with a razor blade, he would be held morally responsible for failing to perform the action of taking away the razor blade, although various sub-acts, such as grasping the child's wrist with one of his hands, moving his other hand into position, etc., would have been required to do so.

In both the situations of the passengers observing a strangler and of the child with a razor blade, the action called for in the circumstances specified may be said to have been obvious to the reasonable person. This may be understood, prima facie, in terms of such assumed principles as: "A collection of persons ought to try to prevent one of its members from being beaten and strangled," and "Adults should try to prevent children from seriously injuring infants." If an additional requirement is made that for the action called for to be obvious to the reasonable person, the desirability and probability of its outcome, compared to the outcomes

[7] Joel Feinberg has considered the variability of possible descriptions: "This well-known feature of our language, whereby a man's action can be described as narrowly or broadly as we please, I propose to call the 'accordion effect', because an act, like the folding musical instrument, can be squeezed down to a minimum or else stretched out. . . . We can, if we wish, puff out an action to include an effect, and more often than not our language obliges us by providing a relatively complex action word for the purpose. Instead of saying Smith did *A* (a relatively simple act) and thereby caused *X* in *Y*, we might say something of the form 'Smith *X*-ed *Y*'; instead of 'Smith opened the door causing Jones to be startled', 'Smith startled Jones'." "Action and Responsibility," in Max Black, ed., *Philosophy in America* (Ithaca, N.Y.: Cornell Univ. Press, 1965), p. 146.

of possible alternatives, must be of a certain level, the requirement can be met in these cases even if this level is set at a high point. And the kinds of action that would have to be taken to prevent the strangling and injuring were in these cases clear.

At this point it should be noted that "reasonable" is not equivalent to "rational." In recent years, the latter term has often been defined as "efficiently self-interested" in the impressive and well-developed literature of game theory and decision processes. "Reasonable," in contrast, has a better chance of retaining an essential moral component, and moralists might do well at the moment to latch onto it, and to hang on.

If, then, the action called for in a given situation is obvious to the reasonable person, it seems that we can sometimes conclude that the judgment "Random collection of individuals *R* is morally responsible for not doing *A*" is valid. *R* could have done something other than non-*A*.

(2) Assume five persons in a train compartment in an old European train. The compartment has a door to the outside. One of the five persons, a doctor, goes for a walk in the corridor, leaving his satchel on his seat. Another passenger, a very large man, begins to have convulsions and, after a few moments, apparently in a frantic search for air, lurches against the door, which opens; he falls out and is killed. The doctor returns, is told by the remaining three persons what has happened, and says, "You should have held him down and administered medicine *x* from my bag." In this case, the desirability and probability of success of the action that the group might have taken, and might only have taken as a group, are again high; a relevant principle, such as "A group ought to try to prevent one of its members from accidentally killing himself," could be assumed without great difficulty; and yet we would not hold the group morally responsible for its failure to perform the action if its members did not, and could not reasonably be expected to, know that the person with convulsions would lurch to the door or that medicine *x* would help him. In this case the action called for was not obvious to the reasonable person, and hence an essential requirement is missing for the judgment "Random collection of individuals *R* is morally responsible for not doing *A*" to be valid. And the doctor's judgment, accordingly, is not a valid moral judgment, because the validity of "*R*

ought to have done A" presupposes the validity of "R was morally responsible for not doing A."

(3) Assume now three unacquainted pedestrians on an isolated street. A small building collapses; a man inside is trapped; he calls to the three for help. He is bleeding from a lower-leg injury and needs immediate assistance. All four persons know that a tourniquet should be applied to his thigh, but this cannot be done until various beams are removed, and removing any would require the strength of all three. The three observers do not agree on how to proceed. Observer$_1$ argues for action$_1$: moving beam$_1$. Observer$_2$ argues for action$_2$: moving beam$_2$. Observer$_3$ argues for action$_3$: moving beam$_3$. While they argue the man slowly bleeds to death.

The situation here depicted was such that any of the proposed actions (plus applying the tourniquet) would have prevented the man from dying. The judgment that "An organized group in these circumstances ought to have done action$_1$, action$_2$, or action$_3$" can be considered valid. But *which* action to take was not obvious to the reasonable member of the random collection; so, again, an essential requirement for holding a random collection of individuals responsible for the nonperformance of an action was missing.

However, it was obvious to the reasonable person in this case that any one of the three proposed actions would be better than no action. The problem was one of deciding which action to take; that a decision between "action$_1$, action$_2$, or action$_3$" was called for *was* obvious to the reasonable person. Hence the random collection can be held morally responsible for failing to make a decision on which action to take—for failing, that is, to adopt a decision method.

As previously stated, a distinguishing characteristic of an organized group or collectivity as opposed to a random collection of individuals, is that the former has a method for deciding to act: it has officials who can act in its name, or a voting procedure to arrive at its decisions, or customary procedures to guide its actions. The possession of such a decision method by a collection of individuals, is, we might say, that which transforms a collection of persons into an organized group or collectivity. In the foregoing example, then, we can say that the random collection of pedestrians was morally responsible for failing to turn itself into an organized group capable of taking action requiring a decision. The judgment, then, that "Random collection *R* is morally responsible for not constituting itself into a group capable of deciding upon an action" is sometimes valid when it is obvious to the reasonable person that action rather than inaction by the collection is called for.

A significant difference between the moral responsibility of a random collection as opposed to the moral responsibility of an organized group is that the former seems to be distributive; that is, if random collection *R* is morally responsible for the failure to do *A*, then every member of *R* is morally responsible for the failure to do *A*, although perhaps in significantly different proportions. In contrast, if organized group *G* is morally responsible for the failure to do *A* it does not follow that member *M* of *G* is morally responsible for the failure to do *A*. If a random collection *R* can be represented as a set equivalent, say, to *M* & *N* & *Q*, then, if *R* is morally responsible, we would seem to be able to conclude that *M* is morally responsible, *N* is morally responsible, and *Q* is morally responsible. On the other hand, if these same members formed an organized group, the group could not be adequately represented as equivalent simply to *M* & *N* & *Q*, because its depiction would have to include the decision method by which the members act as a group, and the distribution of moral responsibility over such a combination would not seem plausible.

This is not to say that because we cannot assign moral responsibility distributively in the case of an organized group, *no* one is morally responsible; for surely decision methods alone are not capable of "acting," but we need to know more before deciding who.[8] Moreover, in saying that the moral responsibility of a random collection is distributive, we may not be saying very much; for if the action is one that could be taken by the random collection only as a group, questions about apportioning responsibility for all the various components of the action, assuming the action

[8] See Stanley Bates, "The Responsibility of Random Collections," *Ethics*, July, 1971.

can be broken down into its components, remain open. But it is to say that everyone in the random collection is morally responsible to some degree.

Seymour Hersh's careful reconstruction of the events which took place during the "attack" on My Lai 4 on March 16, 1968, by the men of Charlie Company, contains the following descriptions:

> Moments later Stanley saw "some old women and some little children—fifteen or twenty of them—in a group around a temple where some incense was burning. They were kneeling and crying and praying, and various soldiers . . . walked by and executed these women and children by shooting them in the head with their rifles." . . .
>
> Now it was nearly nine o'clock and all of Charlie Company was in My Lai 4. Most families were being shot inside their homes, or just outside the doorways. Those who had tried to flee were crammed by GI's into the many bunkers built throughout the hamlet for protection—once the bunkers became filled, hand grenades were lobbed in . . .
>
> . . . Some grenades were also thrown into the ditch. Dennis Conti noticed that "a lot of women had thrown themselves on top of the children to protect them, and the children were alive at first. Then the children who were old enough to walk got up and Calley began to shoot the children."
>
> . . . Le Tong, a . . . rice farmer, reported seeing one woman raped after GIs killed her children. Nguyen Khoa . . . told of a thirteen-year-old girl who was raped before being killed . . .
>
> When Army investigators reached the barren area in November, 1969, in connection with the My Lai probe in the United States, they found mass graves at three sites, as well as a ditch full of bodies. It was estimated that between 450 and 500 people—most of them women, children and old men—had been slain and buried there.[9]

There is no doubt that ignorance, frustration, and the desire for revenge for the killings suffered by their own men contributed to the outbreak of mass shootings engaged in by American soldiers at My Lai. And the general level of brutality and criminality

[9] Seymour M. Hersh, *My Lai 4. A Report on the Massacre and its Aftermath* (New York: Vintage, 1970), pp. 49–75.

in American military practice in Vietnam makes clear that not all the responsibility for the massacre rests with the individuals doing the shooting. Telford Taylor, assessing the massacre in the light of other war crimes, writes that:

> The ultimate question of "guilt" in the trials of the Son My troops is how far what they did departed from general American military practice in Vietnam as they had witnessed it. This may not be germane to the question of legality under the Geneva Conventions or the Articles of War. But the defense of superior orders has its true base not in technicality but in equity, and is properly invoked by the low-ranking soldier in mitigation of punishment for conduct, even though unlawful, that is not too far removed from the behavior authorized or encouraged by his superiors in the force in which he serves.[10]

Nevertheless, to act in disregard of valid moral judgments against domestic murder remains unjustifiable for angry individuals with impulses to kill relatives or strangers, no matter the level of the crime rate. In circumstances where it is obvious to the reasonable person that an action is called for to try to stop such unjustified killing, we would seem to be able to hold a random collection of individuals morally responsible for failing to take such action. To act in disregard of valid moral judgments which at the very least forbid the deliberate, avoidable, and militarily unnecessary killing of unarmed and unresisting persons, including children, remains unjustifiable, no matter the conditions of war. When it is obvious to the reasonable person that attempting to stop such killing is called for in a given situation, we would seem to be able to conclude that a random collection of individuals are to be considered morally responsible for failing to make such an attempt. Of course, an action of attempting to reduce unjustifiable killing does not guarantee success, but it requires that some appropriate sub-acts be taken in furthering the attempt.

That the slaughter of the innocent—in Vietnam and elsewhere—occurs on other levels and wider scales than at My Lai is obvious. The massacre at My Lai makes explicit the moral responsibility of those who could have acted to reduce the awfulness of the massacre and did not. It illustrates the moral

[10] Telford Taylor, *op. cit.*, p. 160.

responsibility of those who could act to reduce unjustified killing on other levels and wider scales and do not. The conclusion to be drawn from reflection on it is not that a greater responsibility excuses a lesser one, but that because it is obvious to the reasonable person that when the innocent are being slaughtered, some action should be taken, the question to be addressed to every person of every random collection faced with such killings is not "did you take part?" but rather "what did you do to stop the slaughter?"

H. D. LEWIS

The Non-Moral Notion of Collective Responsibility

Collective Responsibility

If I were asked to put forward an ethical principle of particular certainty, it would be that no one can be responsible, in the properly ethical sense, for the conduct of another. Responsibility belongs essentially to the individual. The implications of this principle are much more far-reaching than is evident at first, and reflection upon them may lead many to withdraw the assent which they might otherwise be very ready to accord to this view of responsibility. But if the difficulties do appear to be insurmountable—and that, very certainly, does not seem to me to be the case—then the proper procedure will be not to revert to the barbarous notion of collective or group responsibility, but to give up altogether the view that we are accountable in any distinctively moral sense.

On this matter more will be said below. In the meantime, let us

* An earlier version of part of this article appeared under the title "Collective Responsibility" in *Philosophy,* Vol. XXIII, 1948. It is used here with the kind permission of the Editor of *Philosophy,* Lord Acton.

insist that the belief in "individual," as against any form of "collective," responsibility is quite fundamental to our ordinary ethical attitudes; for if we believe that responsibility is literally shared, it becomes very hard to maintain that there are any properly moral distinctions to be drawn between one course of action and another. All will be equally good, or equally evil, as the case may be. For we shall be directly implicated in one another's actions, and the praise or blame for them must fall upon us all without discrimination.

One must admit that the distinction between what is outwardly right and the proper estimation of the worth of persons is not always very clearly drawn in our ordinary ethical thinking. This is very frequently a source of great confusion. The more plainly we draw the distinction between the rightness of the act and the worth of the agent, the more will it also be evident that the main reason for stressing this distinction and the main consideration by which men may be induced to draw it, is that in *addition* to the distinctions we draw between the ethical qualities of actions in their "material" or outward aspect there are even more important distinctions to be drawn in respect of their moral value. We want to be sure that our estimation of moral worth is not prejudiced by considerations relating only to outward action, and it is the former that is usually uppermost in our ordinary ethical judgments. It therefore seems plain that, however prone we may be to confuse the two sorts of ethical judgments which have just been distinguished, we normally have little doubt that some of our actions are better than others, not merely in their effects, or in some other "material" regard, but in themselves and morally. All our usual ethical thinking presupposes this. If it is to be argued that, in respect to properly moral worth, there are no grounds for choosing between the lives of various individuals, then it must be made very plain that this is diametrically opposed to all that we normally think, to the attitudes we adopt from day to day, and to the main body of philosophical reflection on ethical questions.

This may be affirmed without prejudice to the further question of whether it is possible in practice to form reliable estimates of one another's moral worth. Subject to certain limitations, it seems not impossible to assess the moral worth of another person's conduct, and there appear to be some occasions where censure is in order, not merely as directed to outward conduct or as a means of inducing reconsideration of the rightfulness of the course pursued, but as directed to the moral choice itself. But if this is denied, and if it is also held that the difficulties attending the attempt to appraise one another's moral qualities rule out every prospect of success, it by no means follows that the distinctions themselves are suspect. We can know in a general way under what conditions moral censure is incurred without needing to determine how far those conditions apply in particular cases. There is nothing very disconcerting to ethical theory in having to admit, should that appear necessary, that we have no appreciable insight into the strictly moral struggles of other persons (even in the cases of our friends and acquaintances) or no such understanding of the factors involved as would lead to reasonably certain conclusions.

Some comment may be added here on the reliability of the estimates we form of our own moral worth. Is fallibility in this regard also irrelevant to the question of whether there really are moral qualities of conduct? This appears to me to be a most important question, but I will only venture here to make two observations. Firstly, the view which is commonly held, namely that we are usually wide of the mark in attempts to assess our own worth, seems to me very mistaken. To substantiate this in detail I should have to consider the main ways in which moral worth has been conceived. But it must suffice to note the two main alternatives. We may hold that moral distinctions depend mainly on our motives and characters, or we may relate them to some choice or free effort of will not determined by character. If we adopt the latter alternative it seems impossible that anyone should be in doubt about his own moral worth, for no one can really doubt whether he is making an effort to follow the course which his conscience requires. But if we adopt the former alternative there is room for deception of oneself in so far as we may be deluded about our own motives. How far is such delusion possible; how far may a person persuade himself that he is contributing to a hospital from benevolent motives when he is really more concerned to ensure the esteem and gratitude of his fellows? If it is held that we can be widely astray in our understanding of the motives which move us to action, it seems to me that we have here a very formidable argument to advance against the first of the two main alternatives noted above, namely the view that moral worth qualifies character and motives. My second observation is, then, that the nature of properly moral value seems to be such that it would be very strange to ascribe it to features of our conduct which we do not fully understand and bring within our control. To affirm that there can be serious delusion about our own moral attainments is thus, in effect, to cast very grave doubt on the validity of moral distinctions and the reality of moral responsibility.

The belief that we can be mistaken about our own moral worth owes its prevalence in no small measure to failure to distinguish effectively between questions about the "material" rightness of action and the question of the worth of the agent. In respect of the former we are indeed frequently subject to much error and perplexity, and persons of sensitive conscience have often incurred a great deal of mental pain because the very proper concern which they have felt about the "rightness of their act" became the cause of misgiving also about their own moral worth. Yet when the issue is clearly confronted, and it is understood that unavoidable ignorance may not be imputed to the agent, it is hard to see how we can entertain doubts about our own culpability or blamelessness in respect to conduct sufficiently recent for us to retain a clear impression of the way we responded to what seemed to be a duty. Nor is our own impression in matters of this sort easily dimmed in the course of time.

It is in respect to other persons that appraisement of moral worth is difficult, for the factors involved are not easily accessible to the outside observer. But there is no cause for misgiving here because even if we never knew how others fared, our assurance that their actions, like our own, are subject to moral distinctions, would not be a bit affected. Yet if we surrender the view that there are such distinctions, and substitute for it the notion of some uniform moral quality pervading the whole of humanity, or even the whole of a particular group, we are left with nothing which we can recognize as our workaday ethical ideas. Morality has suffered a complete transformation; we seem in fact to have, not morality at all, but the repudiation of it.

The etymology of "responsibility" suggests that it means "liability to answer," this being, of course, liability to answer to a charge, with the implication that if the answer is not satisfactory a penalty will be incurred. This is certainly the meaning of responsibility in the legal sense, and there can be little doubt that the original meaning of the word must be sought along similar lines, for men have not always distinguished clearly between law and morality—in primitive life both are merged in communal custom. But we do not distinguish sharply between them today. It is possible to be legally guilty and morally innocent, and *vice versa*. The question arises, therefore, whether the legal meaning of responsibility provides any analogy to the meaning of the term in the ethical sense. I do not think that it does. It would, no doubt, be easy to point to sanctions which societies impose on their members outside the sphere of State enactment, some of them (for example certain kinds of ostracism), taking very subtle forms; and there are also penalties which individuals are apt to impose on themselves, as recent psychology has shown so well. But these may also be out of accord with ethical requirements. No enactment is morally fool-proof. A man may thus be morally guilty in respect of conduct to which no sort of penalty attaches, and this only helps to bring out in an indirect way what is in fact equally evident in cases where legal or quasi-legal requirements coincide with the moral law, namely that the mere fact of our liability to suffer a penalty is far too incidental a feature of conduct to constitute moral responsibility. Even if we hold, as do the advocates of the retributive theory of punishment, that wickedness calls for infliction of pain on the guilty agent, this is something *further* which we affirm about moral evil and responsibility, and not the essence of them. Such punishment presupposes the evil to which it is appropriate. We may thus reject the retributive theory of punishment, as I would certainly do, without impugning the validity of moral distinctions. What, then, does responsibility mean? It means simply to be a moral agent, and this means to be an agent capable of acting rightly or wrongly in the sense in which such conduct is immediately morally good or morally bad, as the case may be. But what do we mean by rightness, moral worth, and their correlatives? To this no answer is possible, for here we are dealing with ultimate ethical conceptions not reducible to natural fact. The sum of this is that responsibility is an ethical conception not to be defined by reference to ideas which are not themselves distinctly ethical.

Responsibility cannot therefore be conceived in naturalistic terms such as a threat of punishment and our liability to suffer it. But if we overlook this, and come to conceive of moral responsibility in ways not substantially different from our accountability before the law of our State, then it is easy to see how we come also to hold that there are some occasions, at any rate, when we share our responsibility with others and are immediately implicated in their wrongdoing. This happens in the following way. Normally, the purpose served by the imposition of penalties requires the penalties to be inflicted on persons presumed to have offended, and on no others. If punishment were meted out without discrimination, its deterrent effect would be substantially lessened and, for the most part, reversed. Punishment would then have to be regarded as sheer injury or as "an act of God" unrelated to our own volitions, and, while thus little able to hinder crimes, it would often provoke them. There are, however, exceptional cases where expediency requires procedings to be taken against a group as if it were an individual entity. No account will then be taken of the guilt or innocence of individual members of the group. It is in this way that a teacher punishes a class of unruly children when he is not able to discover the real offenders, or when a meticulous apportionment of blame is not practicable. Such procedure may have effect in two ways, either (a) by directly deterring the main offenders or (b) by inducing the class to deal with them in ways not feasible for the teacher himself. The less recourse is had to such measures the better, both from the point of view of effective discipline and from regard to the ill-effects of a lingering sense of injustice. Yet there may also be some compensating factors, such as a deepening of the sense of community, which we might profitably investigate if we were concerned with educational problems or the general question of punishment. Suffice it for the present to note that, as a device for the achievement of practical ends, we have sometimes to accept collective responsibility. This is fully acknowledged in law, where a parent may in some respects be held to account for the conduct of children, or where a society or corporation may be proceeded against as a single entity or person.

Extending our canvas still wider, we have the imposition of

sanctions against a whole nation in the interest of international order, although it is plain that this involves quite as much suffering for the innocent as for the guilty, the former, in a case of this sort, being probably in a very great majority. Reparations and similar measures adopted against an aggressor among nations may also be mentioned here. Such measures may be needed both in the interest of immediate discipline, and as a part of political education, and they may provide means of redress to victims of aggression. But they will involve a great deal of suffering for persons who could not, by any streak of imagination, be held accountable for the culpable acts of the nation, most obviously in the case of infants and babes unborn. Something of this nature is, in fact, unavoidable in most forms of punishment and presents us with some of its most formidable problems. In consistency with his individualism, Locke tried to show[1] that it could be avoided. He urged that, while the participants in an unjust war could fairly be punished with death, there should be no interference with their property, for that would involve a loss to their wives and dependents. But apart from the well-nigh impossible question of apportioning guilt for participation in an unjust war, once the leaders and authors of atrocities have been reckoned with (and that in itself is a notoriously complicated matter), it is obvious that a man's family may be much more seriously affected, even at the economic level, to say nothing of the deeper personal loss, by the death of a parent or husband than by confiscation of property.

In most cases, then, punishment is very likely to fall in some measure on the innocent as well as the guilty. But this unfortunate fact that punishment must sometimes be deliberately inflicted, without discrimination, upon a whole group, serves only to show the limitations of the expedients by which society furthers its ends. Perfect justice is not attainable in practice, and even if measures which we normally consider expedient and just (in spite of their involving the innocent in the fate of the guilty) prove more easily avoidable than we are usually disposed to think, there will always be some intermingling of justice with injustice in human relations under any conditions we can anticipate. But what does this prove? Does it prove that the innocent share in

[1] John Locke, *Of Civil Government,* Part II, Section 182.

the wickedness of the guilty, that the former are morally answerable for the ill deeds of the latter? Surely not. The question needs only to be stated plainly for us to see how foolish it is to allow our view of *moral* responsibility to be affected by imperfections in the ways in which members of society must deal with one another. And yet that is precisely what happens in a great many writings on ethics and jurisprudence, where the ideas of social and collective responsibility are put forward as properly ethical notions under cover of a false analogy with social enactments such as the enforcement of law.

The view that a man is responsible because "he can be called upon to answer" even if it avoids being naturalistic, reverses the proper relation of blame and responsibility, for the latter is prior to the former. Consider also cases where one person takes responsibility for the action of another, such as the case of a Prime Minister taking responsibility for the actions of his Chief of Staff by declaring his "readiness to take the blame." This example serves to show very well on what a misleading course we are set upon when we conceive responsibility in the way described. For a Prime Minister can never be *morally* responsible for the act of a colleague, he simply cannot "take the blame" *morally*. In the conduct of a war, or in the normal functioning of Parliamentary government where, in Great Britain at least, joint Cabinet responsibility seems to be established, it may be necessary for a minister to allow the action of another to be treated as if it were his own. But his willingness to share the blame in this sense, especially if he puts his own position and career in serious jeopardy, induces us to esteem him highly as a moral person even if it is also a reason for seeking to overthrow his administration. His "implication" in the follies or misdeeds of his colleagues is not a moral one, but a requirement of certain governmental procedures, and his loyal acceptance of it, at personal inconvenience, redounds to his credit. It would, of course, be a different matter if he had encouraged or condoned the wrongful policy himself, or if he were sheltering a colleague for personal reasons, or were retaining him against the interest of the public. He would then be morally responsible, but in respect of his own action. It is one thing to accept responsibility for others for practical purposes, to incur certain consequences for what another person has done; to be morally accountable is another. In this last regard we cannot answer for one another or share each other's guilt (or merit), for that would imply that we could become directly worse (or better) persons morally by what others elect to do—and that seems plainly preposterous. Lt. Calley and his company must answer individually for their acts, as shown in the following section.

The belief that guilt may be shared derives some plausibility also from the loose expressions which normally serve our turn when we need to refer to the contributions of several persons to a joint undertaking. Take a case of burglary. We have first the thieves who actually carried it out: one of these may be the prime mover, a confirmed criminal perhaps; another a novice pressed somewhat reluctantly to be his accomplice. The temptation and opportunity may have been put in the way of these two by an acquaintance who bears the victim a grudge but takes no part in the actual robbery beyond supplying useful information. Yet another person may have covered the escape of the criminals or, by hindering the work of detection, have become an accessory after the fact. Finally, we may have a "receiver" who disposed of the stolen goods. Each of these persons is in some way implicated in the crime, and they may thus be said to share the responsibility for it; but it would be a great mistake to suppose that we have here a single criminal operation the blame for which rests equally on all concerned. Even the law would discriminate sharply in such a case, imposing the heaviest penalty on the habitual criminal, but, in his own case as well as that of the others, reviewing the judgment in the light of extenuating circumstances, previous convictions, etc. The instigator who provided the original inducement might easily escape the toils of the law altogether. Still, at the properly moral level many further factors must be taken into account, several of them not easily accessible to the outside observer. In this reckoning many roles may be reversed, the instigator, possibly, proving the worst offender. What has to be stressed is that the guilt of each is strictly proportionate to his part in the joint undertaking. It is not one crime that we have but many.

This seems very evident in the simple case described. It is just as true, however, in respect to complicated matters, such as social and economic injustices, where the lure of vague collectivist explanations is stronger. Reformers have often reminded us that we need not merely to hinder the criminal, but also to remove the causes of crime, and, in this connection, it is frequently maintained that society shares the guilt of the criminal. Consider the case of a poor woman who steals a loaf to feed her starving children. Some will contend that society is really as responsible as the woman herself, in as much as society failed to provide for her needs. They may even go so far as to speak of blaming the social "structure." But that, it seems evident, is only meaningful in a figurative sense and as a rhetorical device when concern is to be aroused at distressful social conditions. If taken in the literal sense it is very misleading, for neither "a structure" nor "society in general" can be the bearer of moral responsibility; these are both abstractions which we must be careful not to hypostatize. What should be said, if we are to speak exactly, is this: the guilt of the poor woman is lessened, if not eliminated altogether, by her circumstances. Yet she alone is to blame, if blame there must be, for what she herself has done. Others are also to blame, but *for something else*—namely, for their part in allowing her to remain in desperate need. They are responsible for this as individuals, and strictly in proportion to what each might have done, directly or indirectly, to ameliorate her lot.

This has a close bearing on the problem of war guilt. This question, it should be stressed, is only one aspect of the general question of the treatment of aggressor nations, for many factors besides that of moral guilt enter into the latter problem. So far as the properly moral issue is concerned, however, we do very serious damage to the prospect of eventual reconciliation if we allow a distorted conception of moral guilt to complicate questions which are already bewildering enough. Thus we would not merely form a wrong estimate of the course we should pursue ourselves, but also encourage those pathological conditions to which vanquished peoples are prone, and which, however they may accord with our mood and the immediate requirements of a situation, are certain, if only by being unhealthy conditions unrelated to any rational assurance, to emerge at a later date in ways very little amenable to rational control—whatever the precise direction they take. What we need to ask, in the case of the United States and the Vietnam war, is not what is the record of the United

States as a nation but just what could have been expected of the average American citizen in the swirling tide of the events which engulfed him and others in the war. This is not to suggest that he was helpless and must be exonerated altogether, or that questions of guilt concern only those who were in positions of power and authority. There were undoubtedly many things which the ordinary citizen might have done, and I can only leave it here for the historian in due course to attempt to determine what they were. But allowance must clearly be made for tradition, outlook, and environment, for the difficulty of anticipating the course of events (and it is easy for us afterwards, and from outside, to be wise about these), for the limited influence which the individual, even if he is of a heroic mould, can normally have on the policies of a government, and for the determined opposition to warlike measures which a certain proportion, at any rate, of the American people showed. Let us seek, by all means, to extend the influence of democratic principles which will enable the individual to give of his best to his State. But in the meantime, let us be fair to him, wherever he is found, by relating the question of guilt not to some abstract entity in which he and all other individuals are merged, but to what we can reasonably estimate could have been expected of the individual, who is the sole bearer of guilt and merit, in the particular situation confronting him, including the massacre at My Lai.

We are most prone to false simplifications of complicated issues in times of confusion and change such as the present. For in such times there is apt to be a recrudescence of primitive ethical attitudes, as the recent history of Europe shows so well. Primitive peoples pay little heed to the individual; the unit is for them the tribe or the family. But reflection upon the affinity between the doctrine of collective responsibility and the undiscriminating "ethic of the tribe" should go a long way to discredit the former.

Failure to take due account of these matters will not only distort our vision in this or that particular regard, but will also poison our human relationships. It will give us, in general, an utterly misleading picture of man and "the human situation." Of this there is ample evidence already in the prevailing fashion of gloomy denunciation of all human endeavor, an indulgence which may show itself before long to be a more serious business than we are inclined to realise. Its immediate progeny are despair and its twin irresponsibility. But worse may follow.

The My Lai Killings

The events which have now come to be known as the My Lai Massacre afford us a remarkable example of the ease with which we may drift from the idea of personal or individual responsibility to the notion of shared or collective responsibility, and thus eventually to no responsibility at all. The first reaction of those who read the account is one of shock, as was made plain in the impact it had at once on public opinion in America and elsewhere. Hardened though we are by now to barbarities of various kinds, we still find it difficult to realize that they continue and are perpetrated by seemingly normal members of highly civilized societies. We have no immunity in modern war; sanctions and starvation have little respect for nice distinctions, and bombs do not always fall on military targets. We believe this notionally, but we absorb the reports as we take them in through our casual glance at the newspapers, without letting the belief become a real one. And then something happens, thrusting the full horror of what is done through the subtle defences which we build up to preserve the normality of daily existence. When this happens we react with almost stubborn disbelief—"It just can't be! How could anyone do such things in a deliberate calculated way? If it really did happen, how can ordinary educated people lapse into such appallingly wicked and cold blooded cruelty?" Thus moral indignation mounts, and we comfort ourselves and perhaps congratulate ourselves that we "are not as other people." It is impossible that we should do what Lt. Calley did, and we turn the shock into the luxury of indignation. We are all set to denounce and censure.

This is not a new frame of mind. No one can fail today to be aware of terrible barbarities perpetrated in our times in many parts of the world besides Vietnam. But by dint of thrusting Hiroshima and Nagasaki out of our minds, or regarding them as special cases, we are apt to go on blandly assuming that these are things that other peoples do, peoples that have succumbed to authoritarian regimes or who have been possessed for the time by some curious demon of unreason. Millions of Jews were slaughtered in one way or another under Hitler, many of them herded into concentration camps to starve or await their turn for the gas chamber. The brutality in Hungary was the work of communists; it would not be allowed in our name.

One astounding fallacy in all this is the failure to realize that, in normal contexts and encounters, the Germans who were "caught up" in the Hitler regime and peoples in countries beyond the iron curtain, are not all that different from ourselves. The cultural achievement of the German people is beyond dispute; they have come generally within the same civilizing influences as ourselves, they are an eminently Christian community; and, while there are features of their history which we do not share, in essentials there is more that is common than different. If these things could happen to such civilized and gifted people as the Germans—and note how we slide into speaking of "happen" rather than "be done"—why not in somewhat different conditions by ourselves? But before we know where we are, with the spectacle of being arraigned in the same way before a moral tribunal ourselves, we begin to speak of "conditions" of "historical forces" and "social upheavals" which will bear for us on their impersonal shoulders the burden of the guilt incurred. In particular the plea of ignorance comes to the fore. How many people, we ask, really knew what was going on in Germany, and what chances had they of knowing before it was too late and the iron bands of a ruthless tyranny were clamped upon them? Go back to the desperation of the Weimar Republic, the frustration and humiliation; consider how a strong ruler would present himself as exactly what the nation wanted to pull itself together and restore its dignity and place in the world. Incidental injustices there might be, but something of the kind is inevitable if great things are to be done. You cannot expect your hands to be altogether clean in an imperfect society, and look how much is gained in other ways.

This is how many people thought in the early days, and once the new regime was firmly on its way, no one was very clear what was happening. There was threat of war and the menace of encirclement, and thus it came about that people who would normally deal with one another in fair and considerate ways found themselves in effect acquiescing in practices as barbarous and savage as any that have stained the pages of history. It was not directly their doing; they gave no commands; they carried out no tortures themselves; and even those who were directly involved in various atrocities—sometimes, we are told, quite gentle and affectionate people in their families—were carrying out instructions for which the responsibility lay elsewhere. If there was fault it was the fault of national policy, and if there was a disease it was a disease of the whole German people. Events had overwhelmed them, and a certain latent element of unreason in their culture and history had been given a rare opportunity to extend itself. What could the ordinary citizen do, caught up in the turmoil of these events and the passions they aroused? Hindsight is all very well for us, but what could the ordinary citizen do to arrest the terrible march of the Juggernaut in the middle thirties—or earlier? What could the citizens of other communities do, many of them thoughtlessly enjoying their colorful holidays down the Rhine and romantic tours of German cities?

Some, in fact, did do a great deal. It is not likely that so many Jews could have escaped and established themselves elsewhere without considerable help from outside, on occasion provided at considerable risk. Many German citizens were martyred; the churches, somewhat belatedly on the whole, voiced their protest; and we learn of remarkable people with no outstanding gifts or position, like Franz Jäggerstatter,[2] clearly discerning the duty of resistance and paying the terrible price of responding to it. Their efforts had little impact on others; if they were admired it was more for their courage than their understanding and many of them just disappeared from the scene except for the grieving hearts of their families. The rest were caught up in the confusion and momentum of events, more sinned against than sinning and thus the responsibility shifted from the uneasy shoulders of individuals to the community, the state, society, the march of events—anything, in fact, which makes it easier for us not to carry a burden of guilt ourselves. The climax of this was the German confession of guilt initiated by the German churches after the war and implicating all in virtue of just being Germans,

[2] See *In Solitary Witness* by Gordon Zahn (New York: Holt, Rinehart & Winston, 1964).

even those who were much too young to have any idea of what was happening—even babes unborn.

This fitted in well with much that was uppermost in German theology at the time, and especially the doctrine of universal sin. Some seemed to take a masochistic delight in vilification of themselves, not primarily for anything they had actually done themselves but for the evil state of man as exhibited in the revival of barbarous practices. These views were much echoed elsewhere and the idea gained ground again that man is in fact wholly evil, though some of the outward effects of his actions are good. There is "a more or less" in the outward effect of actions but there is no "big sinner" or "little sinner," for what we have to deal with is the terrible sinful state of man. There is a remedy for this at the spiritual level, but none, it seems, that will make a difference to our persistence in a sinful state here and now.

A peculiarly extravagant version of this confused and pessimistic view appeared in a Christian news-letter book by D. R. Davies and was much commended by no less a person than Archbishop William Temple.

"History (i.e. trying to live in defiance of God's will) is a mug's game . . . Whatever originates from the will of man remains self-destructive . . . But in the ruins of each illusion, man, with an optimistic determination worthy of a better cause, rises to a fresh illusion, which in our day, happens to be socialism of one kind or another. Socialism, if it is ever tried, will be no more successful than its historic predecessors in overcoming the basic contradiction of human nature. Nothing human can ever do that. But let man try. That is why God has made man free. He will discover it won't work . . . The civilizations of the past must all be viewed in this way as lessons in the futility of human effort . . . They ran the gamut of origin, rise, development and decay, all of which constitute a single process in successive phases. It is a process in which inherent contradiction matures to final destruction." And in the more recent examples the process comes to its climax with greater rapidity, for "God is becoming impatient. The Holy Ghost is in a hurry."[3]

[3] D. R. Davies, *Divine Judgment in Human History* (New York: Macmillan, 1943), pp. 19–20.

We shall not dwell on the appalling intellectual confusion, to speak of nothing else, disclosed in this particular passage, or to weigh again the baneful influence in this way of much theological thinking in our time. But such a passage should promote the disturbing awareness that today we are again in danger of falling into substantially the same sort of confusions, whatever the role of theology in the process. This is well shown in the bemusement of our attitudes towards the events at My Lai and similar occurrences. The events themselves are not in serious doubt, any more than we can doubt today the horrors, on a massive scale, of the concentration camps. A number of simple people, few of whom could have had any understanding of the issues involved in the Vietnam War, and who were not obviously combatants at all, were deliberately hounded into a ditch and done to death. Pleas for mercy went unheeded, surrender was not allowed, and among the victims were many who could not by any means be thought to be combatants, if only because they were very young children. These actions go against all the rules of war, such as they are, and against all feelings of humanity and mercy. There is no doubt, on the evidence made available, that Lt. Calley and others did these things, and it is certain that there have been many similar cases in Vietnam of brutality and savage maltreatment. The court found Lt. Calley guilty on various counts.

It is when we think in this way that we become furiously indignant. Horrified denunciation takes its course; when we avert the eye of our imagination from the scene at My Lai to the solitary figure in the Court Room in Georgia, a somewhat different sort of compassion begins to stir. Calley, and his associates, were after all soldiers under orders in a peculiarly confused situation. Soldiers must do as they are told. How else can a war be fought? The ordinary soldier does not know how the battle as a whole is being fought; that is for commanders and generals. It may have seemed to many soldiers in the First World War that the mass slaughter in the trenches in France availed very little for either side, but no one stops to blame them for it; the decisions on the conduct of the battles were not for them. No more did Calley decide strategy in Vietnam. It was moreover jungle war. As the Court was told, you rarely see your enemy in the jungle; the slightest stirring may mean the menace of instant death; the enemy is not always in uniform, and even tiny children are trained to take part, even to the extent of throwing grenades or leading patrols through the minefields. It is not clear that Lt. Calley was expressly told to "waste" the village, but he was clearly being pressed to hurry on with the task generally assigned to his force and get to his objective. His experience in this kind of warfare was not long, and there is indication that he had blundered in a crisis in his civilian employment. If governments expect wars to be fought in these conditions and if fairly raw youths are suddenly plunged into the worst of it, what can one expect? Scruples are easily observed from an armchair, not so easily in the jungle; and the demoralizing effect of jungle war today, where your next step may let off a booby trap or find you in a deadly ambush, hardly needs stressing. Inured to the butchery of war, armed with weapons which can instantly kill a large number of people, is it any wonder that hapless and innocent people become the victims of a ruthless drive to an urgent objective with as little cost to one's own forces as possible?

This is how the defense goes, and many people have been almost as indignant at the humiliation and privations of Lt. Calley as others have been about the slaughter at My Lai. To many it seems unreasonable, and indeed gravely unjust, to send young American citizens to Vietnam to fight in conditions of the greatest horror and confusion, and then hold them to account for incidents which are inevitable features of the kind of war to which they are sent. And if this does not lead, as it did with many, to a complete whitewashing of all that happened, it does put the events in a very different perspective; we tend then to wonder whether anyone is in fact to blame. If blame is in order at all we tend to shift it from those directly involved to their superiors, and from them to the politicians, and from them to the present state of the community, to "us all," or indeed to the state of the world at the present time and the course of history. The buck is no longer being passed; it does not come to rest, even on the desk of the President, and it has just disappeared into a morass of hypostatized abstractions. The state of the world is the state of no one in particular; it is far removed from anything you or I may do from day to day.

How then can we avoid the compulsive logic which seems to take us from fierce denunciation to an almost total dissolution of moral, or indeed any other, accountability? Only by understanding better what moral judgment involves. Morally a person is judged according to his rights. Ignorance exempts. But is there no culpable ignorance? Not if it is invincible, in the traditional term. It is, however, a duty to make ourselves as well-informed about what we ought to do as we can; we need to keep our consciences clear and alert as well as to obey them. Some are more conscious than others of the duty to discover what is our duty in this or that regard, and sound education should produce citizens who are morally alert in this way. We are not all of us equally conscious of this duty, and the fault may lie partly in our own past. Though it is not always a person's fault if he or she is not as morally sensitive as others, it is at the same time hard to believe that reasonably intelligent people are quite unaware of the duty to find where exactly their precise duties lie. This is a matter of opportunity and also of degree. Some start with a better endowment and a more sensitive conscience than others, but the degree of moral turpitude varies with other factors also, such as circumstance and state of mind. The main point for us is to avoid the extremes of supposing that moral situations present themselves simply in black and white. It is for every man to judge his duty and do what he can in the situation that confronts him.

Lt. Calley could not stop the Vietnam war. Nor could he alter the character of it. That does not mean that he and other citizens had nothing to do with it. If a country is at war, it is everyone's duty to consider whether the war (and, indeed, any war at all) is just and unavoidable, and also to consider whether certain features of the war as conducted may not be improper even if the war itself is just. The action we should then take will depend on the views we form; and the way we bring our opinions to bear on the policies adopted in our community will also vary much with the nature of those opinions and our own endowment and opportunities. Though everyone does not have the nature and opportunity to be a radical reformer, it does not follow that there is nothing we can do, even if we cannot bring about extensive changes.

There is evidence that Calley had not been entirely unmindful of these obligations of a citizen, but these obligations could hardly have entered his thoughts on that terrible day at My Lai. It was a crisis, and speedy action had to be taken in the urgent military situation in which he found himself. Was it wrong to kill the villagers whom he had ordered to be driven to the ditch, or have them killed? Everyone would say it was, irrespective of any view about the war itself. Admittedly, non-combatant villagers could be a menace, and, granted the state of war as it developed at My Lai, there was need to move forward speedily with as little danger as possible to the troops involved. Yet it is hard to believe, in the light of the evidence, that the military situation afforded no alternative to the immediate slaughter of all villagers, regardless of age or sex, or even that slaughter was in order at all. To kill unresisting civilians in this way, especially when they were quite separate from combatants, is opposed to all sensible policy and to all the conventions of war. Nothing in the urgency of the military situation seems to rule out the alternative of keeping the prisoners under guard, or, if they could not be guarded, of taking what risk was involved (in this case it seems a slight one) of leaving them unhindered where they were. Opinions may differ on this issue, but even allowing for the confusions of jungle warfare, the reports do not suggest that military necessity at the time required the villagers to be immediately slaughtered. Short of a policy of killing all civilians at sight in an area of jungle warfare (and a war that involved this would have another terrible mark notched up against it), there seems to be nothing to justify the killing at My Lai. This judgment stands, however hard we may strain ourselves to make all allowances, as we feel much impelled to do, at our comfortable distance of space and time.

Even if we say that the deed itself was not required by the military situation, what of the orders given to Lt. Calley? Here the evidence is not altogether clear. Was Lt. Calley expressly told to "waste" the village? On this the evidence is conflicting. If the answer is "yes," that is certainly a considerable extenuation of any guilt that remains with Lt. Calley himself. Legally, the position may be hard to determine. What is the legal obligation to obey an order that is not legal in itself? Morally, a junior officer *might* be largely, if not wholly, exonerated if there were an unambiguous order from a superior source. But much still depends on the nature of the order, for even if there is no question of the war itself not being just, there could still be circumstances in which it would be proper, and indeed obligatory, to disobey the order. This must always be a difficult decision, but there is clearly a general right of the citizen to resist the state, even to the point of disobedience. That right is not abrogated in time of war. The conditions which warrant this extreme measure must be very exceptional in democratic states where the normal instrument of change is persuasion and where constitutional procedure is usually more important than righting a particular wrong. Even in an army in time of war, where prompt obedience is paramount if the war is to be fought at all, there can yet be orders which deviate so much from moral principle that one is entitled, nay obligated, to disobey them.

If the orders were to slaughter non-combatants not in any immediate line of combatant fire—to do this to men, women, and infants, regardless of the kind of physical and mental distress that occasioned them—then there seems to be a good case for saying that here the soldier and the pacifist could join in saying, "No." There are things which a just war does not warrant. Atrocity is still atrocity, and no soldier can surrender his conscience entirely to his officers, however just the ultimate cause. But was Lt. Calley aware of this? In the urgency of his mission and the tension of the kind of engagement in which he was involved, did he realize that what he was doing was morally atrocious? Had he time to weigh the pros and cons of disobedience? How far was his judgment dimmed or numbed by tension and anger at all that had befallen his comrades? These are much harder questions to answer, and on this point there will no doubt be much sharper difference of opinion.

Even when again we make all the allowances, one would expect the citizen of a civilized state to realize that the massacre of the villagers at My Lai, in the circumstances as we are able to establish them, passed beyond any warrant which the exigencies of war are bound to lend to much that is otherwise naked cruelty. At the same time, the temptation to brush aside scruple, to take the line of least resistance, to let the greater strains of pity be muted in the day to day acceptance of harsh realities, would also be strong; and, if the orders were explicit, to summon up the courage to disobey with the battle in progress would require much clarity of vision as well as moral resolution.

In the light of these considerations, how we should pass judgment on any individual is a moot point. To assign blame is one thing; to determine the extent of it quite another. Moral turpitude is not a case of just standing on one side or the other of a sharp division, whatever the theologians may say; there is a big sinner and a little sinner, and how much anyone is in fact morally at fault is a matter which only he himself and his Maker can decide. Not that we are quite at a loss. We know when we are grievously at fault and when only slightly so. We may know this of others too, within limits. But any precise estimation of moral good or bad, in cases other than our own, is precluded for us by the sheer inwardness of much that is vital. Simply we do not know the whole story, and it is doubtful whether, even in our own case, we can see it clearly when the tide of further events, especially a long trial and public controversy, has swept over it.

There is one further point that must be stressed. Any guilt which Lt. Calley, or any other soldier, incurred at My Lai was his own. He must answer for just what he did as he understood the situation. No one else can be held to account for that, or for any part of it. The actions of others affect the situation, and they may provide vital extenuating considerations, but what Lt. Calley did he did. If at fault the fault was his; and if his associates were at fault with him they were each at fault according to the situation that confronted them and their own understanding of it. Those who did the most outward harm need not be the most evil in the sight of God. How it looks to God is not for us to judge, though this does not mean that we should withhold all moral censure. Proper moral indignation, by contrast with condemnation of the outward deed, must be tempered by the provisional and imperfect character of our assessments.

Does this mean that all others are exempt, that Lt. Calley and his associates at the time must bear all the guilt for all that happened at My Lai? In a way, yes. If they were to blame, *they* were to blame for what they did. But this does not mean that others were not involved morally in the situation in which the soldiers found themselves at the time. The guilt of many others may indeed be greater. If Lt. Calley was ordered to "waste" the village and everyone in it, the guilt of whoever gave the order could well be greater. Even here again, though, nothing is just black and white; much depends on how the situation developed and how it presented itself to the superior commander. How much discretion did he mean to give to his juniors, did he intend the slaughter to proceed regardless of resistance and in the absence of obvious menace, and was he including the women and children as well? To what pressures and confusions was he subject in turn? If he was to blame, he was to blame for what *he* intended as he understood the situation, for what *he* did or failed to do.

Likewise as we draw further away from the actual scene of the killing itself. No one could complete the tally of all who had some part in bringing about the situation which confronted the soldiers at My Lai—some in positions of great prestige and influence, some more humbly, some in a military role, some as civilians, some well past the age of any active participation in the conduct of the war. They were all involved, some in good ways, some in bad. But this is just where we must be careful, for no one is involved beyond the sort of thing which it was open for him to do. Many would have had things to do which were closely concerned with the mission on which Lt. Calley was sent; others would be involved in arrangements made more remotely or in the general conduct of the war and related policy. The ordinary citizens, engaged in their daily business, would have nothing to do directly with the conduct of the war, much less with particular incidents in it. Still, they would be involved in other ways. They can vote, they can take part in the formation of public opinion, they can make efforts to understand situations like the Vietnam War and see what contributions they can make to the ending or ameliorating of it. Some have gifts which enable them to do more than others in these ways. But no one can absolve himself of the duty to do something, if only to play his general part in democratic life more effectively—or to do more good where he can, whether concerned with public policies or not. Neglect of these duties could affect in various ways the situation in which Lt. Calley found himself. The quality of life of a community has repercussions on most aspects of it, and the difficulties in which the soldiers found themselves in the jungle—even the fact that they were there at all—may be due to, or at least aggravated by, easygoing concern with one's own interest or the greedy preoccupation with personal gain in his political attitudes by the citizen at large.

And not just American citizens. It is idle to say today that the Vietnam War is solely the concern of the American people. It is the concern of us all, not just because it has repercussions on our own interests, but because of humanitarian claims to which all are open. There is much to be done in other countries besides those which happen to be at war, some of it concerned with the creation of an alert and sensitive conscience about war and the conduct of war, some concerned with general conditions of our life today as they affect problems of war and peace and other problems. The influence of one individual may appear slight, and many are deterred by this thought. Yet the cumulative effect of the way we all live is great, and we should not despise the day of small things.

Attainment or neglect of these levels could well be reflected in a particular situation like that at My Lai, and this could affect, perhaps by way of considerable extenuation, the guilt of the persons involved at the time. However, in our eagerness to take this into account, we must not conclude that the actual guilt of those who took part in the massacre itself is shared by others. The action of others, as affecting their circumstances, may affect their own guilt. But they remain accountable for what they did in the situation as it affected them; others are accountable for their own conduct in the varying situations in which they in turn found themselves. To think otherwise is to blur the issue; it induces us to spread the genuine responsibility of the soldiers over the life of the entire community, and indeed over present day society as a whole, in such a way that it disappears from sight altogether. The corresponding responsibility of all of us, in our several stations, likewise is eroded. *Where all are responsible no one is responsible,* thus we tend to lapse into a state of moral indifference or aquiescence which can be one of the greatest ills to afflict a society. In the confusion and perils of our social existence today there are few things that need to be kept more persistently and firmly in our minds than the fact of our personal responsibility in all the situations in which we may find ourselves. The renewal of the sense of personal responsibility, in private as in public concerns, is a very urgent need of our time.

The excuses of Tomlinson[4] will not do for us any more than they did for him at Heaven's Gate:

"Stand up, stand up now, Tomlinson, and answer loud and high
"The good that ye did for the sake of men or ever ye came to die—
"The good that ye did for the sake of men in little earth so lone!"
And the naked soul of Tomlinson grew white as a rain-washed bone.
"Oh, I have a friend on earth," he said, "that was my priest and guide,
"And well would he answer all for me if he were at my side."
—"For that ye strove in neighbour-love it shall be written fair,
"But now ye wait at Heaven's Gate and not in Berkeley Square:
"Though we called your friend from his bed this night, he could not speak for you,
"For the race is run by one and one and never by two and two."

[4] "Tomlinson," *Rudyard Kipling's Verse,* Vol. 11, p. 158.

STANLEY BATES

My Lai and Vietnam: The Issues of Responsibility

OUR INITIAL RESPONSE to learning of the events which occurred at My Lai is to feel the impotence of philosophizing about them and to turn away from them in revulsion, disgust and shame. Surely there are no "philosophical" issues to be debated here; one is confronted with sheer horror, and the only human reactions to it—outrage, desire to see the guilty brought to justice, compassion for the victims—need not be mediated by a conceptual analysis, but ought simply to be expressed. But subsequent to My Lai itself we also have the spectacle of the national reaction to it and to the trial of Lieutenant Calley, a reaction best described by the title of a study of it—*My Lai: It Never Happened and Besides, They Deserved It.*[1] We have further the charade of military legal proceedings against those most intimately involved in the atrocity and in the Army's cover-up of it. We have suggestions that all of us are somehow guilty, so that no one should be singled out for punishment.

[1] Opton and Duckles, *My Lai: It Never Happened and Besides, They Deserved It* (Berkeley: Wright Institute, 1970).

In order to gain a clear understanding of what an appropriate reaction to My Lai would be, it does seem necessary to investigate the tangled issues of individual and collective responsibility. This paper will not attempt a detailed discussion of the facts of this particular case or an assessment of the responsibility of particular individuals in the perpetration of the atrocity which occurred on March 16, 1968. (These are important issues, but they need to be investigated in detail by reporters, detectives, historians and, indeed, have been.)[2]

MORAL AND LEGAL RESPONSIBILITY

This paper will be concerned chiefly with the issue of moral responsibility. The obvious fact that moral and legal responsibility are not coextensive implies that each will have its peculiar problems. There are important questions of legal responsibility raised by My Lai. For example, there has been a good deal written about the issue of whether the Nuremberg precedent shows that the United States has committed itself to the legal enforcement of the prohibitions against crimes against peace, war crimes, and crimes against humanity, all of which, it might be argued, the U.S. has committed in Vietnam.[3] There is also the question of command responsibility for an atrocity such as My Lai under the Yamashita precedent. (General Tomayuki Yamashita was condemned by a U.S. military commission and executed for war crimes committed by troops under his command even though he had not approved or ordered these actions and there was "no evidence that he knew of them other than the inference that he must have because of their extent."[4] One problem with these legal issues is that technical disputes tend to overshadow the original issues of

[2] For example, in Seymour M. Hersh, *My Lai 4: A Report on the Massacre and Its Aftermath* (New York: Random House, 1970).

[3] The best general discussion of legal aspects of the war-crimes issue is Telford Taylor, *Nuremberg and Vietnam: An American Tragedy* (New York: Quadrangle Books, 1970). One should also see Richard Wasserstrom's review of Taylor's book in *The New York Review of Books,* 3 June 1971, and Richard Wasserstrom, "The Relevance of Nuremberg," *Philosophy and Public Affairs,* Fall, 1971.

[4] Taylor, *op. cit.,* pp. 91–92.

concern. What is the status of a "law" of war? What, indeed, is the status of an international law? A second problem is that answering a question of legal responsibility may not be sufficient to answer a question of moral responsibility. Take the Yamashita precedent. Suppose that we established that it is a valid principle of U.S. military law, and that according to that principle General Westmoreland, the commander in Vietnam at the time of My Lai, ought to be legally condemned. We may still think that the precedent is itself morally wrong, that General Yamashita ought not to have been executed—and that his case by itself cannot provide a morally good ground for holding General Westmoreland legally responsible for My Lai. Responsibility implies "liability to certain responsive attitudes, judgments, or actions."[5] Legal responsibility implies liability to certain determinate, authoritative, institutional responses. Moral responsibility implies liability to a variety of responses for which the criterion of appropriateness is much less clear in nature. We shall investigate this a bit more later.

There are certain assumptions which provide the background of this paper: that morality is actual, that moral distinctions are real distinctions, and that propositions expressing moral judgments and the ascription of moral responsibility are capable of truth or falsity. Let us also assume that men are capable of choosing among alternatives, the alternatives themselves often being limited by factors which are out of the control of particular individuals. It may seem grotesque to call these "assumptions," since they seem to be clearly true and to be common features of everything that can be called "moral." Indeed, they seem to be preconditions of the meaningfulness of moral language, not merely of its applicability. Note also that they are not assumptions about the correctness of a particular moral view, but rather assumptions about morality itself and about human nature.

The remainder of this paper consists of three sections. The first deals with features of individual and collective responsibility. The second section discusses the issues of individual and collective

[5] Joel Feinberg, *Doing and Deserving* (Princeton: Princeton University Press, 1970), p. 222.

responsibility for My Lai and for the Vietnam war with respect to three different groups—soldiers, national leaders and ordinary citizens. In conclusion is a discussion of a number of responses to the My Lai massacre which seem to involve fallacious inferences.

AN ANALYSIS OF RESPONSIBILITY, INDIVIDUAL AND COLLECTIVE

The term "responsible" is used in ordinary language in such a way that we can be responsible for good as well as bad deeds, for morally praiseworthy as well as morally blameworthy actions. However, let us restrict our analysis of responsibility to those cases in which those who are responsible are in some degree blameworthy.

In the ordinary case, where we ascribe responsibility to an individual for a blameworthy act certain conditions must have been met for our judgment to be justified. Joel Feinberg suggests three such conditions.

> First, it must be true that the responsible individual did the harmful thing in question, or at least that his action or omission made a substantial causal contribution to it. Second, the causally contributory conduct must have been in some way faulty. Finally, if the harmful outcome was truly 'his fault', the requisite causal connection must have been directly between the faulty aspect of his conduct and the outcome. It is not sufficient to have caused harm and to have been at fault if the fault was irrelevant to the causing. We can use the expression 'contributory fault' to refer compendiously to these three conditions. Thus, in the standard case of responsibility for harm, there can be no liability without contributory fault.[6]

Feinberg is speaking more in a legal context than a moral one here, but these conditions still provide a convenient starting point for us (particularly because he goes on to discuss the deviations from this standard case which occur in legal cases of collective responsibility). One addition that we might make to Feinberg's condition is that for a person to be responsible for a deed, it must be the case that he did it voluntarily. The topic of voluntary action is a notoriously difficult one, which we cannot pursue here.

[6] *Ibid.*

(As Austin has shown, it is related to the topic of excuses.[7] It may be that an adequate excuse sometimes relieves a person of direct responsibility, or that it shows that his action was not voluntary—therefore not one for which he should be held responsible.) There are standard ways of explicating the statement that "he acted voluntarily," e.g. "he could have acted otherwise," which don't seem to me to increase our understanding very much. Fortunately, our understanding doesn't need to be helped here. We all have a sufficiently reliable set of intuitions about what "voluntary" means to proceed (and it is these very intuitions which are the bases of philosophical analyses on the subject). We also know the kinds of things that excuse one from moral responsibility: "I didn't know that it was his coat; I thought it was mine"; "I had to break the promise or he would have killed my children." These considerations are simply an amplification of the second condition that Feinberg lists. To say that a person's contributory conduct was "faulty" may be in part to say that he acted voluntarily and in the absence of excusing conditions.

The concept of collective responsibility has received a bad name in the twentieth century. Even those who believe it to have been an historical necessity that at certain times men and women in a given collective should have been held responsible for the deeds of others in that same group, they did tend to believe that it was a mark of progress to have dropped this practice. Twentieth century reversions to this practice—for example, the Nazis' murder of Jews simply because they were Jews, the killing of hostages, and reprisals in wartime—seem to be reversions to barbarism. However, there *are* plausible reasons for the incorporation of certain variants of the concept of collective responsibility in most contemporary legal systems. Feinberg treats collective responsibility, which is "any liability for which the contributory fault condition is weakened or absent,"[8] as simply a sub-species of strict liability. The arguments in favor of certain kinds of strict liability in the civil law are impressive. People who engage in extremely hazardous activities are put on notice

[7] The best starting point for recent philosophical discussion of excuses is J. L. Austin, "A Plea for Excuses," reprinted in J. L. Austin, *Philosophical Papers* (New York: Oxford University Press, 1961).

[8] Feinberg, *op. cit.*, p. 223.

that they must be prepared to compensate anyone injured by their activities even if the activities are carried on carefully, with all precaution, and without "fault." The argument in favor of this is that it permits the activities to be carried out rather than outlawed and that it permits those who carry them out to know in advance what their risks are. One can also find some intuitively acceptable examples of strict liability in the criminal law, even with criminal penalties. Again, the arguments in favor of vicarious liability (where the contributory fault is ascribed to one party, and the liability to another) in certain forms in the civil law are quite strong. Feinberg's examples are in the areas of the use of authorized agents: the responsibility of superiors in certain hierarchical organizations for the actions of those under their command or supervision; the responsibility of an employer for an employee's actions (within limits); and the responsibility derived from suretyship, as in the case of a bonding company which will make good the losses incurred due to a defaulting employee. In all of these cases there is a very plausible rationale for the practice of ascribing vicarious liability, though it seems plausible *not* for liability to punishment, but only for liability to rectification and compensation.

It is appropriate to mention these cases where there is some form of strict liability because of the bad name that the concept of collective responsibility has acquired. We tend to think of examples like blood feuds or Nazi extermination programs when we think of collective responsibility. To punish a man simply because he is a member of some group, even if the group has done something wrong, goes against our fundamental moral views if the individual is without contributory fault. (This is the main reason that most people who are not lawyers are morally outraged when they come to understand the nature of conspiracy laws in our own legal system. This is one of the most obvious places in our law where legality and morality differ.) Most of the cases where there is a plausible rationale for strict liability of the kind involved in collective responsibility are *not* cases in which punishment is involved. If we can ascribe a similar moral responsibility in these sorts of cases where there is no question of formal sanctions, the following question then must be raised: to what sort of responses is the morally responsible person appropriately liable?

There is no easy answer to this; nor should we expect one. One of the advantages of the law is its determinate character—the nature of the penalties is set, the penalties are prescribed, and where flexibility in the assessment of penalties is permitted, it is flexibility within certain prescribed limits.

Once we, individually, have made moral assessments, it is not so clear how we are to act on them. Our actions are limited by morality itself, and they generally need to be limited, too, by a healthy sense of our own fallibility. If we believe someone to have been guilty of a war crime, or responsible for a war crime, we may simply have no occasion for further action, or we may decide to dissociate ourselves from the person, or to oppose actively the awarding of honors to that person. We may try to publicize our judgment and to get others to agree with us. There is no clear, simple answer to the question of what we should do in the absence of a fairly comprehensive account of our circumstances, obligations, and opportunities. We, as individuals, are not in a position to punish, except in the extended sense of punishment in which our disapproval and its negative consequences for the person of whom we disapprove count as punishment.

Our example of vicarious liability included the case of hierarchical organizations. In organizations in which a strict discipline is maintained, such as in military units, it is important to make superiors liable for the actions of their subordinates. This is one way in which superiors acquire a real incentive to maintain the performance of those under their command at the highest possible level. If a military unit is slack, inefficient, and fails in various ways to fulfill its responsibilities, the commander of that unit ought not to be able to relieve himself of responsibility by pointing out that he did not order, or intend, that the unit should be slack, inefficient, and irresponsible. However, the fact that the commander must (within limits) bear responsibility for the actions of his subordinates does not, by itself, imply that the subordinates have no responsibility for their own actions. This is entirely clear in the cases in which their actions are either not in conformity with, or are in violation of, commands which their superiors have issued (even if they, very realistically, did not believe that the commands would be enforced). The less clear case is one in which a subordinate is asked to bear responsibility for an action which he took in conformity to an order from a superior. Here it is obvious enough that the superior must be held responsible for the actions which he ordered; it is less apparent that the subordinate ought also to be held responsible for his action. Often in war-crimes trials, the defense, based on the concept of "superior orders," attempts to take advantage of our intuitive ambivalence about this situation. After all, the man was only obeying orders.

In this century, Adolf Eichmann is the best example of why this defense cannot be allowed to provide a general excusing condition for behavior which has been ordered. Eichmann told the court in Israel that all of his activities pursuant to the goal of the extermination of the Jewish race had been taken under orders. It is clear that there are actions so heinous that no order to take them should be obeyed. This is explicitly recognized in the military codes of most countries. For example, the U.S. Army field manual of 1956 says:

> The fact that the law of war has been violated pursuant to an order of a superior authority, whether military or civil, does not deprive the act in question of the character of a war crime, nor does it constitute a defense in the trial of an accused individual, unless he did not know, and could not reasonably have been expected to know that the act ordered was unlawful.[9]

Note that it might seem possible to interpret the moral liability of the superior as being derived ultimately from some contributory fault of his own. One could say that what the superior officer did (or perhaps did not do) was responsible for X, where X is to be understood as some contributory factor to the subordinate's having performed a blameworthy act. Thus, in the case of General Yamashita, it could be argued that what General Yamashita was really responsible for was not the particular war crimes which troops under his command perpetrated, but rather that he was responsible for "the breakdown of troop discipline" which was in turn at least a necessary condition for most of the particular war crimes which did occur. Thus, though his liability for those particular war crimes was vicarious, it was based on his actual

[9] F.M. 27–10, *The Law of Warfare,* p. 182, par. 509, entitled "Defense of Superior Orders" quoted in Taylor, *op. cit.* p. 51.

liability for the non-performance of his duty. Of course, the whole point of the concept of vicarious liability in the law is to relieve the prosecution of the onus of establishing the condition of contributory fault. However, if there is to be any moral justification for the practice of assessing liability vicariously, it must rest on some such ground as I have just put forward—that there is fault, but that it is only indirectly related to the ultimate blameworthy act, and perhaps it is not causally related to the blameworthy act.

Let us now make some brief general comments about the concept of collective responsibility.[10] Most of us are aware, at a phenomenological level, of the very complex ways in which we are related to our families, to our communities, to our nations. These complex phenomena are not well-accounted for by our traditional model of how men are related in society. This traditional model is embodied in what might be called the main line of liberal-democratic theory. It represents society as an aggregation of sovereign individuals. The fundamental reality is the individual—the individual as "isolated monad," to borrow Marx's phrase.[11] In the contract tradition, either society itself or, more modestly, political society, is seen as the outcome of a bargain struck by rational, self-interested individuals. Now this can be an immensely illuminating way to proceed in analyzing some of the basic concepts of political theory, particularly the case with regard to the concept of rights. However, it is possible to confuse what an individual has a right to do with what it is right for an individual to do. The right of the individual to liberty, insofar as it has been achieved, is a precious and precarious historical accomplishment. One of the things which a theory of individuals' rights seeks to establish is that an individual can have a (political) right to do something which is morally wrong for him to do. Nor does this show a fundamental conflict between political and moral theory; it rests simply on a conception of the appropriate limits of the state's power to coerce.

[10] I draw in part on a very fine recent article, W. H. Walsh, "Pride, Shame, and Responsibility," *The Philosophical Quarterly,* January, 1970, pp. 1–13.

[11] T. B. Bottomore (Ed.), *Karl Marx: Early Writings* (New York: McGraw Hill, 1964), p. 24.

We are related to others in many ways beyond our common status before the law, and some of these ways may involve us in moral relationships that are not covered very well by the liberal democratic model. For example, we may feel some special attachment to the place where we live, so that if we hear our home city being described as ugly, dirty and dull, we may get very defensive about it. If I am from San Francisco, and I meet a fellow San Franciscan at a convention in Dallas I may feel a special bond with him, even though I have never seen him before.[12] Similarly, I may cheer for athletic teams which represent my city, and take pride in their victories, and feel sorrow in their losses, even though I, as an individual, have nothing at all to do with them. I may find myself cheering for U.S. athletes at the Olympic Games, and in some way I count their accomplishments as mine. I may think of my country's history, taking pride in certain accomplishments, and at the same time feeling ashamed of the barbaric destruction of native American Indian culture. Why should these events of the historic past affect me at all?

Without postulating a theory here which purports to explain these and similar phenomena, let us note that the conception of an "individual" existing apart from, and prior to, a social structure is a myth. (Of course, a physical human being, a single individual could be raised entirely apart from human society. However, he would not only fail to develop into a complete human being, lacking such crucial attributes as language, but probably at a certain point he would even lose the capacity to become a human being.) We are implicated with others in myriad ways, many of which we don't even suspect, and very few of which are freely chosen. The language we speak, the institutions which shape our lives, the customs and culture which form us and others, are not freely adopted by us even though they are conventional in nature. Moreover, these things determine the range of our available options of ways of life. We choose, where we do, among limited opportunities. It is no wonder that we have fellow feelings

[12] David Hume, in L. A. Selby-Bigge (Ed.), *A Treatise of Human Nature* (New York: Oxford University Press, 1968), p. 482, says, "We love company in general; but 'tis as we love any other amusement. An *Englishman* in Italy is a friend; A *European* in *China*; and perhaps a man wou'd be belov'd as such, were we to meet him in the moon."

for those who are in the same, or fairly much the same, position that we are.

All of this is relevant to one sense of "collective responsibility." We may feel the distinctively moral feelings—righteous indignation, guilt, pride, shame—about acts with which we as individuals have no connection at all. The heinous acts of our own country are closer to us than the heinous acts of some other nation. I may be outraged by some of the acts of the Germans in World War II; I do not, however, feel the personal shame with respect to them that I do with regard to many of the things which the United States has done in Vietnam. (Perhaps an individual of German descent would feel more involved in German guilt.) Of course, my shame doesn't show that I am blameworthy, or that I ought to be punished for those heinous acts. It does, though, indicate to me that I *ought* to do something about Vietnam, and that if I now take no action at all, I will have some personal contributory fault not for the war in Vietnam or any particular war-crimes, but, perhaps, for the apathetic state of U.S. public opinion about the war. Though we have emphasized there the negative feelings of guilt and shame, one should add that, unless a person is liable to these negative feelings when he judges that his country has violated some standard of morality or failed to live up to some moral ideal, then that person is not capable of genuine pride in his country's accomplishments and is unable to take genuine pleasure in its positive achievements. The possibility of pride and the liability to guilt and shame are simply two aspects of one situation—a fundamental involvement in the life of the nation.

VIETNAM: THE RESPONSIBILITY OF SOLDIERS, NATIONAL LEADERS AND ORDINARY CITIZENS

Let us turn now to a more particular discussion of the responsibility of various groups of U.S. citizens for My Lai and for certain general features of the Vietnam war. The classes that I have in mind are: soldiers in the field, leaders of the war effort (especially civilian architects of the war), and ordinary citizens.

The case of the soldiers in the field seems relatively clear. Soldiers, like all human beings, are morally responsible for the actions they take in the circumstances in which they find themselves. The soldiers who were active in the commission of crimes at My Lai are morally responsible (and legally responsible, though most won't be held legally responsible) for what they did. Even if they were ordered to commit atrocities, the orders were illegal. Thus, the particular men who raped the women of the village, who killed the old women and children, who herded people into a canal and then murdered them in cold blood are guilty of terrible crimes. Each individual is responsible for the particular things that he did; he is not responsible for what others did (unless perhaps he issued illegal orders to others to commit crimes). Those men who did not enter into the murder, rape, and pillage which took place that day are not guilty of *those* crimes. They may, however, be responsible for certain omissions or other action. Did they do anything to prevent the occurrence of the crimes which they must have witnessed? Did they attempt to save any of the victims of these crimes, or to ease the suffering of these victims? (There are occasional stories which relive briefly the horror of My Lai. But the actions of Warrant Officer Hugh C. Thompson, a helicopter pilot who managed to save some lives at My Lai, stand in sharp contrast to the activities of almost everyone else at the scene of the atrocity.[13] Did they, after the event, make any effort to see that justice was done? The Vietnam veteran whose questions touched off the investigation that led to the public revelations of what happened at My Lai described his own reaction to his discovery of what had happened there. "I wanted to get those people. I wanted to reveal what they did. My God, when I first came home, I would tell my friends about this and cry—literally cry. As far as I was concerned, it was a reflection on me, on every American, on the ideals that we supposedly represent."[14]

An important factor in our judgments about the actions of the men at My Lai is our assessment of the degree to which the situation of being an infantryman in Vietnam excuses the actions which they took. This factor has been very heavily emphasized in the discussions of the My Lai massacre. None of the ordinary soldiers on the scene had, in any sense, freely chosen to be there. Our army in Vietnam is a conscripted army, and our system of military recruitment has insured that the burden of actual combat

[13] For the Thompson story, see Hersh, *op. cit.*, pp. 61–66.
[14] *Ibid.*, p. 105.

operations falls most heavily on those from the lowest economic position in society, on the racial minorities of America, and on those with the most limited educational background. The nature of the guerrilla war which is being waged by the National Liberation Front guarantees that the distinction between the civilian noncombatant population and enemy troops will be an extremely difficult one to apply on the battle-field. In any case, our troops have been given inadequate instruction in the laws of war, and the laws of war unrealistically require an ordinary soldier in the field to make a complex judgment about the legality of the orders which he has been given.

These are the sorts of considerations which are urged, by some, as reasons for not holding ordinary soldiers responsible for acts such as those committed at My Lai. Though one could not say that these considerations are irrelevant to our judgments, a very careful consideration of the nature of their relevance should be undertaken. In a legal setting such considerations would *not* tend to show that a crime had not been committed; rather, they would perhaps be considered as justifying a mitigation of the punishment which would ordinarily be given for the crime in question. Similarly, in our assessment of moral responsibility, where we have already said that there is a great unclarity about what practical action is to flow from our moral judgments, these considerations cannot be thought by anyone to *justify* the acts at My Lai; they may be thought to provide some *excuse*. Of course, no one can have thought that bayonetting infants or massacring women, old people and children was morally permissible in any circumstances. In reading about the reactions of those who took part in the atrocity, one is struck by the way in which their memories of My Lai haunt many of them.

There have been other massacres and other atrocities in Vietnam. However, the kind of incident which occurred at My Lai was not the standard practice of the U.S. Army. It is important to realize that a war crime may be committed even though none of the particular actions of ordinary soldiers on the scene may be war crimes. For example, the U.S. practice of relocating noncombatant civilian populations in Vietnam is a war crime.[15] The establishment of so-called free-fire zones—and the subsequent

[15] See especially Chapter 6 in Taylor, *op. cit.*

practice of shooting any person found in the zone—is a formula for the production of war crimes. However, the ordinary soldier who aids in the relocation of civilian population may commit no war crimes at all. Here, as in all cases of judgments of moral responsibility, we need a very precise description of that action, policy, or situation for which the moral responsibility is being assessed. The ordinary soldier obeys orders and performs particular actions which are required by the policy of relocating the civilian population. However, he may not even know that the actions which he is performing are being taken to implement this policy. We cannot correctly say of him that *he* is relocating the civilian population. The individuals responsible for this particular war crime are those who have helped formulate the policy and put it into effect. Here we come to the second group whose moral responsibility should be considered—the military and civilian leaders who are responsible for the war in Vietnam.

It would be very difficult to assign responsibility at the highest level for particular atrocities such as My Lai. Perhaps it could be shown that the general policies of waging the war had promoted a climate of contempt for the local Vietnamese population and that this climate made some such atrocities inevitable. It almost certainly could be shown that the military practice of judging the success of operations in terms of body count helped produce My Lai. The responsibility of particular officers such as Colonel Barker, Colonel Henderson, Captain Medina, and Lieutenant Calley for what happened at My Lai seems capable of assessment. The real issue of the moral responsibility of the architects of the Vietnam war is their responsibility for what *they* did—not their responsibility for the individual violations of the laws of war by ordinary soldiers. It is important, as I have already mentioned, to get a correct description of what they did do. This is not always easy to do, since one of the victims of the war has been the English language. It is no accident that a kind of Orwellian Newspeak has been consistently employed by those with the responsibility for Vietnam. One merely has to think of the war crimes committed in the name of "pacification" to have a clear example. Think also of the phrase "protective reaction strikes" used to describe U.S. bombing raids on North Vietnam. It will take some time before an independent assessment of the actions of our leaders in formulating and executing the policies which produced Vietnam will be possible. We have enough preliminary information from sources such as the Pentagon Papers to know that, in general, our leaders were perfectly well aware of the nature of the actions which they took. Interestingly, if one accepts an analysis of the war as an inevitable consequence of American "imperialism," or as the accidental outcome of a number of reasonable and morally permissible actions taken by men of good will, in either case one will tend to judge the individual actors in the creation of the Vietnam war less harshly than someone who believes their individual actions were morally wrong and that it was quite possible to know that they were morally wrong.

Here, with leaders as with ordinary soldiers, I don't think that a real question of collective responsibility arises. Each individual is to be held morally responsible for his own actions. The real questions of collective responsibility are raised by the situation of the third class of people whom I want to consider—the ordinary citizens. To what extent can either particular atrocities or the general conduct of the Vietnam war be considered the moral responsibility of an ordinary American citizen who has neither participated in the formulation of war policies nor in any actual acts of war? First, in regard to particular atrocities, one may feel shame as an American that Americans have done these things without also feeling responsible for them. Atrocities, which are not a part of official policy, are not done *in the name of us* as American citizens. They are particular violations of the rules of war committed by particular individuals. Only if there is a strong *argument* presented which tends to show that an atrocity is not simply the product of individual aberration but is rather a manifestation of an official, or semi-official, policy does it seem to me that the question of collective responsibility is appropriately raised. For what am I responsible, or for what should I feel guilty? Suppose that I have never been interested in foreign policy, and that I have never really paid very close attention to what my government has been doing. Is this sufficient for me to establish my non-involvement with the war in Vietnam? The answer seems very clearly to be—no.

We cannot require of any ordinary citizen that he do something which has an actual effect on the policies of his government. One of the political lessons of the 1960's is the incredible difficulty of affecting government policy. We can, however, believe that the ordinary conditions of citizenship require that people become aware of what their government is doing and make some attempt, however small, to influence the government. After all, there has been a large peace movement in this country (although it consists of a quite small percentage of the population), and it can justifiably claim to have had some influence on the evolution of American public opinion on the war which, in turn, has had an influence, albeit a slow one, on government policy. Surely, one consequence of this is that those who were in any way active in their opposition to the war do not share in the responsibility for it. (Of course, if they were only symbolically washing their hands of involvement, this would not be enough to relieve them of responsibility.) However, the converse may also be true: that for a suitably described group of American citizens, their failure to oppose the war is sufficient to involve them in the responsibility for it and to make appropriate a special feeling of guilt on their part.[16] I say "suitably described" because it does seem that there are some conditions which must be met in order for someone to be a member of this group. For example, one would have to be capable of understanding the issues involved in the war and to have sufficient access to the news media to be informed about the facts of the war, the immediate past of Vietnam, the proposed justifications of U.S. policy, etc. It doesn't seem too difficult to understand the kinds of conditions which are relevant.

We have throughout presupposed and not argued that the moral judgment of what the United States has done in Vietnam must be a negative one, and in that context have tried to suggest the conditions under which a judgment of shared responsibility for the war might be made, even though an individual had no direct contributory fault to the war at all. Speaking about racism in American society, Martin Luther King, Jr., once said, "We will have to repent in this generation not merely for the vitriolic words and actions of the bad people, but for the appalling silence

[16] These issues are discussed in: Virginia Held, "Can a Random Collection of Individuals Be Morally Responsible?" *Journal of Philosophy,* 23 July 1970, pp. 471–81, and Stanley Bates, "The Responsibility of 'Random Collections,'" *Ethics,* July, 1971, pp. 343–49.

of the good people."[17] Unfortunately, this is also true of the Vietnam war.

FALLACIOUS INFERENCES ABOUT MY LAI

In conclusion, our discussion addresses responses to the question of making moral judgments about My Lai and about the war in Vietnam. These responses are fairly common, and they are based on certain mistakes which should be exposed.

First, people often say that war crimes are an inevitable accompaniment of war. The crimes of Vietnam therefore present no special problems for the U.S. conscience. But while it is true that some war crimes (such as looting and raping) do seem, inevitably, to accompany any large military campaign, large scale massacres of civilian populations do not belong to this category. They have occurred infrequently in history, which is one reason why their occurrence is so traumatic. It would seem that they could not occur in the absence of quasi-official approval, or the expectation of quasi-official approval, by those who order and commit this kind of atrocity. But what is the atmosphere which permits the existence of such an expectation? One element of this atmosphere is the endemic racism of the American military and of American society. It is expressed in the words of one of the participants at My Lai who said, "It was pretty disgusting, but it was a different feeling. If they had been Americans," he said of the dead Vietnamese, "I might have felt different. I never really understood those people."[18] It is expressed in the words of a military lawyer who described the unwritten M.G.R.—"the mere Gook rule." He explained that the expression had been adopted facetiously by some Army legal officers who believed that military courts were lenient to Americans who killed Vietnamese civilians because the Vietnamese were regarded as somehow second-class human beings or "mere gooks."[19] Surely these attitudes raise problems for the U.S. conscience. And, of course, even if crimes as bad as these were inevitable, they would be inevitable in part because of moral

[17] Martin Luther King, Jr., "Letter from Birmingham City Jail," in Edward Kent (Ed.), *Revolution and the Rule of Law* (Englewood Cliffs, N. J.: Prentice-Hall, 1971), p. 21.

[18] Hersh, *op. cit.*, p. 89.

[19] Taylor, *op. cit.*, p. 162.

faults which need to be exposed. Such inevitability cannot be used as an excuse.

A second response is to assert that our enemy has committed war crimes just as bad as My Lai—especially in regard to the N.L.F program of assassinating those who politically cooperate with the Saigon regime. One thing to be pointed out about this response is that there is a difference between the massacre of a non-combatant civilian population and a revolutionary campaign directed against a regime regarded as imposed from the outside. One cannot say that this does, in fact, justify all the killings perpetrated by the N.L.F. There has been too much purported "justification" of murder in the twentieth century. However, we do regard the activities of the French resistance against Nazi collaborators, or of Yugoslav, or Czech partisans against the Nazis as potentially justifiable. Justification ultimately depends on the overall issues about which the war is being contested—but no overall issue justifies the slaughter of the innocent.[20] The more important response to this supposed equation of the enemy's actions with our own is that, even if it is correct, it cannot justify what is morally unjustifiable. The fact that others are guilty of crimes does not change the nature of the crimes that have been committed by us.

A third response that is often made is that these factors imply a kind of moral self-righteousness on the part of the person making moral judgments. It is easy to make moral judgments sitting at a desk, but the actions we are judging occurred in the heat of combat. Sometimes people add, "If you had been there you would have done the same things they did." Vietnam veterans may be ashamed of some of the things they did, but they tend to resent intensely the judgments of those who weren't there and who don't really know what it was like. It may be true that if any of us had been at My Lai with Charlie Company, we might have committed crimes just as they did. While we may hope that this is not true, one doesn't know the measure of his strength or weak-

[20] There is an excellent discussion of this in Elizabeth Anscombe, "War and Murder," in Walter Stein (Ed.), *Nuclear Weapons: A Catholic Response* (New York: Sheed, 1961), pp. 45–62. The essay is also printed in Richard Wasserstrom (Ed.), *War and Morality* (Belmont, Calif.: Wadsworth, 1970), pp. 42–53.

ness in these matters until it has been tested. However, most American troops usually were not committing atrocities of the nature of My Lai, and there were individuals at My Lai who refused to join in the massacre. The issue here is different from the general issue of the responsibility of the ordinary soldiers for the policies which he helps to execute. Generally, the responsibility for those war crimes belongs to the leaders who have formulated the illegal policies, not the executants. In any case, the fact that I might have done the same thing had I been there does not disqualify me as a judge. It ought to make me aware of all the circumstances that the soldiers faced, and these circumstances are, of course, a factor relevant to any moral judgment which we make of their actions. If an issue of punishment arises, it might help mitigate punishment if it can truly be said that they cannot reasonably have been expected to behave differently from the way they did.

We are sometimes told that only in America are we free to criticize our government and its policies, as though the existence of this freedom precluded the possibility of its ever being appropriately exercised. The truth is that our country requires a continuous criticism by its citizenry (this is, of course, true of other countries as well). Patriotism can be regarded as simply the blind adherence to the policies of whoever happens to hold the reins of government. So regarded, it becomes a purely descriptive category fitting the fanatical Nazi and failing to justify his actions. True patriotism can, however, be regarded as having a moral component; it can be thought of as the requirement to support what is good about our country and to fight what is bad about it. So regarded, true patriotism may require severe criticism of the policies of those in power, for only those liable to guilt and shame for their country's shame can be said truly to love their country.

Related Documents

THE RIDENHOUR LETTER

Mr. Ron Ridenhour
1416 East Thomas Road #104
Phoenix, Ariz.
March 29, 1969

Gentlemen:

It was late in April 1968 that I first heard of "Pinkville" and what allegedly happened there. I received that first report with some skepticism, but in the following months I was to hear similar stories from such a wide variety of people that it became impossible for me to disbelieve that something rather dark and bloody did indeed occur sometime in March, 1968 in a village called "pinkville" in the Republic of Vietnam.

The circumstances that led to my having access to the reports I'm about to relate need some explanation. I was inducted in March 1967 into the U. S. Army. After receiving various training I was assigned to the 70th Infantry Detachment (LRP), 11th Light Infantry Brigade at Schofield Barracks, Hawaii, in early October, 1967. That unit, the 70th Infantry Detachment (LRP), was disbanded a week before the 11th Brigade shipped out for Vietnam on the 5th of December, 1967. All of the men from whom I later heard reports of the "Pinkville" incident were reassigned to "C" Company, 1st Battalion, 20th Infantry, 11th Light Infantry Brigade. I was reassigned to the aviation section of Headquarters Company 11th LIB. After we had been in Vietnam for 3 to 4 months many of the men from the 70th Inf. Det. (LRP) began to transfer into the same unit, "E" Company, 51st Infantry (LRP).

In late April, 1968, I was awaiting orders for a transfer from HHC, 11th Brigade to Company "E" 51st Inf. (LRP), when I happened to run into PFC "Butch" Gruver, whom I had known in Hawaii. Gruver told me he had been assigned to "C" Company 1st of the 20th until April 1st when he transferred to the unit that I was headed for. During the course of our conversation he told me the first of many reports I was to hear of "Pinkville."

"Charlie" Company 1/20 had been assigned to Task Force Barker in late February, 1968 to help conduct "search and destroy" operations on the Batangan Peninsula, Barker's area of operation. The task force was operating out of LZ Dottie, located five or six miles north of Guang Nhai city on Vietnamese National Highway 1. Gruver said that Charlie Company had sustained casualties; primarily from mines and booby traps, almost every day from the first day they had arrived on the peninsula. One village area was particularly troublesome and seemed to be infested with booby traps and enemy soldiers. It was located about six miles northeast of Guang Nhai city at approximate coordinates B.S. 728795. It was a notorious area and the men of Task Force Barker has a special name for it: they called it "Pinkville." One morning in the latter part of March, Task Force Barker moved out from its firebase headed for "Pinkville." Its mission: destroy the trouble spot and all of its inhabitants.

When "Butch" told me this I didn't quite believe what he was telling me was true, but he assured me that it was and went on to describe what had happened. The other two companies that made up the task force cordoned off the village so that "Charlie" Company could move through to destroy the structures and kill the inhabitants. Any villagers who ran from Charlie Company were stopped by the encircling companies. I asked "Butch" several times if all the people were killed. He said that he thought they were, men, women and children. He recalled seeing a small boy, about three or four years old, standing by the trail with a gunshot wound in one arm. The boy was clutching his wounded arm with his other hand, while blood trickled between his fingers. He was staring around himself in shock and disbelief at what he saw. "He just stood there with big eyes staring around like he didn't understand; he didn't believe what was happening. Then the captain's RTO (radio operator) put a burst of 16 (M16 rifle) fire into him." It was so bad, Gruver said, that one of the men in his squad shot himself in the foot in order to be medivac-ed out of the area so that he would not have to participate in the slaughter. Although he had not seen it, Gruver had been told by people he considered trustworthy that one of the company's officers, 2nd Lieutenant Kally (this spelling may be incorrect) had rounded up several groups of villagers (each group consisting of a minimum of 20 persons of both sexes and all ages). According to the story, Kally then machine-gunned each group. Gruver estimated that the population of the village had been 300 to 400 people and that very few, if any, escaped.

After hearing this account I couldn't quite accept it. Somehow I just couldn't believe that not only had so many young American men participated in such an act of barbarism, but that their officers had ordered it. There were other men in the unit I was soon to be assigned to, "E" Company 51st Infantry (LRP), who had been in Charlie Company at the time that Gruver alleged the incident at "Pinkville" had occurred. I became determined to ask them about "Pinkville" so that I might compare their accounts with PFC Gruver's.

When I arrived at "Echo" Company, 51st Infantry (LRP) the first men I looked for were PFCs Michael Terry and William Doherty. Both were veterans of "Charlie" Company, 1/20 and "Pinkville." Instead of contradicting "Butch" Gruver's story they corroborated it, adding some tasty tidbits of information of their own. Terry and Doherty had been in the same squad and their platoon was the third platoon of "C" Company to pass through the village. Most of the people they came to were already dead. Those that weren't were sought out and shot. The platoon left nothing alive, neither livestock nor people. Around noon the two soldiers' squad stopped to eat. "Billy and I started to get out our chow," Terry said, "but close to us was a bunch of Vietnamese in a heap, and some of them were moaning. Kally (2nd Lt. Kally) had been through before us and all of them had been shot, but many weren't dead. It was obvious that they weren't going to get any medical attention so Billy and I got up and went over to where they were. I guess we sort of finished them off." Terry went on to say that he and Doherty then returned to where their packs were and ate lunch. He estimated the size of the village to be 200 to 300 people. Doherty thought that the population of "Pinkville" had been 400 people.

If Terry, Doherty and Gruver could be believed, then not only had "Charlie" Company received orders to slaughter all the inhabitants of the village, but those orders had come from the commanding officer of Task Force Barker, or possibly even higher in the chain of command. PFC Terry stated that when Captain Medina (Charlie Company's commanding officer Ernest Medina) issued the order for the destruction of "Pinkville" he had been hesitant, as if it were something he didn't want to do but had to. Others I spoke to concurred with Terry on this.

It was June before I spoke to anyone who had something significant to add to what I had already been told of the "Pinkville" incident. It was the end of June, 1968 when I ran into Sergeant Larry LaCroix at the USO in Chu Lai. LaCroix had been in 2nd Lt. Kally's platoon on the day Task Force Barker swept through "Pinkville." What he told me verified the stories of the others, but he also had something new to add. He had been a witness to Kally's gunning down of at least three separate groups of villagers. "It was terrible. They were slaughtering the villagers like so many sheep." Kally's men were dragging people out of bunkers and hooches and putting them together in a group. The people in the group were men, women, and children of all ages. As soon as he felt that the group was big enough, Kally ordered an M-60 (machine-gun) set up and the people killed. LaCroix said that he bore witness to this procedure at least three times. The three groups were of different sizes, one of about twenty people, one of about thirty people, and one of about forty people. When the first group was put together Kally ordered PFC Torres to man the machine-gun and open fire on the villagers that had been grouped together. This Torres did, but before everyone in the group was down he ceased fire and refused to fire again. After ordering Torres to recommence firing several times, Lieutenant Kally took over the M-60 and finished shooting the remaining villagers in that first group himself. Sargeant LaCroix told me that Kally didn't bother to order anyone to take the machine-gun when the other two groups of villagers were formed. He simply manned it himself and shot down all villagers in both groups.

This account of Sergeant LaCroix's confirmed the rumors that

Gruver, Terry and Doherty had previously told me about Lieutenant Kally. It also convinced me that there was a very substantial amount of truth to the stories that all of these men had told. If I needed more convincing, I was to receive it.

It was in the middle of November, 1968 just a few weeks before I was to return to the United States for separation from the army that I talked to PFC Michael Bernhardt. Bernhardt had served his entire year in Vietnam in "Charlie" Company 1/20 and he too was about to go home. "Bernie" substantiated the tales told by the other men I had talked to in vivid, bloody detail and added this. "Bernie" had absolutely refused to take part in the massacre of the villagers of "Pinkville" that morning and he thought that it was rather strange that the officers of the company had not made an issue of it. But that evening "Medina (Captain Ernest Medina) came up to me ("Bernie") and told me not to do anything stupid like write my congressman" about what had happened that day. Bernhardt assured Captain Medina that he had no such thing in mind. He had nine months left in Vietnam and felt that it was dangerous enough just fighting the acknowledged enemy.

Exactly what did, in fact, occur in the village of "Pinkville" in March 1968 I do not know for *certain,* but I am convinced that it was something very black indeed. . . .

Sincerely,
/s/ Ron Ridenhour

THE CHARGE AGAINST LT. CALLEY

Violation of Article 118 of the Uniform Code of Military Justice:

Specification 1 In that First Lieutenant William L. Calley, Jr., US Army, 40th Company, The Student Brigade, US Army Infantry School, Fort Benning, Georgia (then a member of Company C, 1st Battalion, 20th Infantry) did, at My Lai 4, Quang Ngai Province, Republic of South Vietnam, on or about 16 March 1968, with premeditation, murder four Oriental human beings, occupants of the village of My Lai 4, whose names and sexes are unknown, by means of shooting them with a rifle.

Specification 2 . . . with premeditation, murder an unknown number, not less than 30 Oriental human beings, males and females of various ages, whose names are unknown, occupants of the village of My Lai 4, by means of shooting them with a rifle.

Specification 3 . . . with premeditation, murder three Oriental human beings whose names and sexes are unknown, occupants of the village of My Lai 4, by means of shooting them with a rifle.

Specification 4 . . . with premeditation, murder an unknown number of Oriental human beings, not less than seventy, males and females of various ages, whose names are unknown, occupants of the village of My Lai 4, by means of shooting them with a rifle.

ADDITIONAL CHARGE:

Specification 1 . . . with premeditation, murder one Oriental male human being, an occupant of the village of My Lai 4, whose name and age is unknown, by shooting him with a rifle.

Specification 2 . . . with premeditation, murder one Oriental human being, an occupant of the village of My Lai 4, approximately two years old, whose name and sex is unknown, by shooting him with a rifle. Specifications 1 and 3 were dropped prior to the court-martial.

THE HAGUE CONVENTION ON LAND WARFARE, 1907

Article 4 Prisoners of war are in the power of the hostile Government, but not of the individuals or corps who capture them.

They must be humanely treated.

All their personal belongings, except arms, horses, and military papers, remain their property. . . .

Article 22 The right of belligerents to adopt means of injuring the enemy is not unlimited.

Article 23 In addition to the prohibitions provided by special Conventions, it is specifically forbidden . . .

(b) To kill or wound treacherously individuals belonging to the hostile nation or army;

(c) To kill or wound an enemy who, having laid down his arms, or having no longer means of defense, has surrendered at discretion;

(d) To declare that no quarter will be given;

(e) To employ arms, projectiles or materials calculated to cause unnecessary suffering; . . .

(g) To destroy or seize the enemy's property, unless such destruction or seizure be imperatively demanded by the necessities of war;

(h) To declare abolished, suspended, or inadmissible in a court of law the rights and actions of the nationals of the hostile party. . . .

Article 25 The attack or bombardment, by whatever means, of towns, villages, dwellings, or buildings which are undefended is prohibited. . . .

Article 28 The pillage of a town or place, even when taken by assault, is prohibited. . . .

MINUTES FROM THE INTERNATIONAL CONFERENCE ON MILITARY TRIALS*

London, 1945

A documentary record of the negotiations of the Representatives of the United States of America, The Provisional Government of the French Republic, the United Kingdom of Great Britain and Northern Ireland, and the Union of Soviet Socialist Republics, culminating in the agreement and charter of the International Military Tribunal.

Mr. Justice Robert H. Jackson for the U.S.A.
Professor Gros for the Provisional Government of the French Republic
Sir David Maxwell Fyfe for the United Kingdom
General Nikitchenko for the U.S.S.R.

JULY 2, 1945

MR. JUSTICE JACKSON. I understand the Soviet memorandum to reject the possibility of trying organizations. The American proposal is that we utilize the conspiracy theory by which a common plan or understanding to accomplish an illegal end by any means, or to accomplish any end by illegal means, renders everyone who participated liable for the acts of every other and in connection with that to utilize these closely knit voluntary organizations as evidence of a conspiracy. That is a rough way of describing our proposal. That is the heart of our proposal. Without that it means

* A Department of State Document.

many trials, which we are not set up to engage in. To my mind, rejection of this plan leaves nothing of our proposal as to organizations which is really worth considering. Therefore, it seems to me that we should give some consideration, before it is rejected, to its merits and to any possible alternative.

These organizations constitute the means through which, under the American proposal, a large number of people can be reached with a small number of long trials—perhaps one main trial.

Some of them perhaps ought to be tried individually on charges of individual criminal actions; but also they should be tried for their part in the planning of extermination of minorities, the aggressive warfare, the atrocities against occupied nationals, and offenses of that character. We think this should be done in a single effort so far as the collective guilt is concerned.

PROFESSOR GROS. Actually, very divergent opinions have been expressed on the question of organizations. We studied the new American memorandum and again the Soviet's objections and have endeavored to understand these divergent views, and we shall try to suggest ways to reconcile them.

First, what are the facts which we are discussing? Countless crimes have been committed by those organizations during the war—the Gestapo groups, S.S. Systematic criminal activities have been committed against the peoples of the occupied countries of which two of these delegations can speak from personal knowledge, and systematic criminal activities have been going on for years. These systematic criminal activities are no accident. The association of those groups was not accidental. These gangs in many localities were tied by one allegiance to a major organization—Gestapo, S.S., S.A., or others. If we want to reach the major war criminals, these major organizations must be our target. On that first point I cannot really see a divergence of views between the American and Soviet suggestions on the facts.

Now, as Mr. Justice Jackson said much better than I would be able to say, if we do not try these organizations as organizations, what will be the situation? I propose to suggest that it would not be satisfactory in the interest of the Four Powers nor in the interest of the United Nations to fail to try them. I submit that war criminals will not be punished merely under the declaration of Moscow or of Yalta. They should be punished even without those two declarations. They should be punished because they merit punishment of war criminals, and those two declarations are only reaffirmation of the principles of international law. But the question of application remains completely open and the declaration of Crimea, as I read it, has little significance by its own terms—"We are determined to . . . bring all war criminals to just and swift punishment . . ."

I will insist again on those terms of the declaration. We are committed to bring all war criminals to justice, and we cannot take those words as a legal pronouncement but only as a declaration of intentions reserving all question of application. . . .

We do not think of it as punishing equally all members of the organization, but the situation would be more like this: First, if a special crime is alleged against one of the members, a special trial will be put against him in the local court or in the occupation court. Second, if, on the contrary, certain supposed members can prove that they are not members of the organizations, that they had no knowledge of the purposes of the organizations, that they had been forced into membership, then they could probably be discharged. Third, in the case of other members against whom no special crime can be proved or who cannot prove their innocence, the organization would in a sense be what the British call "outlawed", and we do not insist upon the kind of punishment that would be applied to them. It might even be decided by higher authorities. . . .

Such collective crimes are known in the French system of law and in the Belgian system of law, and we may be making a mistake but I think also in the Soviet system of law—crimes committed by gangs. What we demand is, in fact, the application by the International Military Tribunal of the same process of charging and punishing gangs. I know that in those systems of law trials are required against members before punishing them, but we consider that the trial of 10 or 15 leaders of an organization is the trial of all the organization and leave open for the rest of the members the question of individual punishment. If we do not try to find any solution, we will be back to the difficulty of letting them go or of punishment without trial at all.

GENERAL NIKITCHENKO. The basic question is the responsibility of organizations and whether it is possible to get a legal declaration by the court that organizations are criminal. The view that the Soviet Delegation has excluded the possibility of the trial of members of organizations for criminal participation in the work of such organizations is not correct.

The Soviet law, criminal law, fully recognizes in exactly the same way as the French, and probably others, the collective responsibility of members of an organization for the crimes committed by the organization. The theory of the Soviet criminal law fully recognizes the trial of gangs or organizations and the responsibility of the members of such organizations in addition to any individual responsibility they may carry for individual acts. Where we do not agree is in the idea that the trial of organizations should form actually the basis of the agreement for the trial of criminals. An organization is not a physical body, but the members of that organization are physical, and, if they have committed individual crimes as members of the organization, then they should be tried individually as physical persons who have committed acts because they were members of a criminal organization.

In order to establish the criminal nature of the criminal actions of the organizations, in the opinion of the Soviet Delegation, it is necessary to investigate the actions of individuals of the organization and to establish the fact that they have committed criminal acts by virtue of their adherence to the organization. How otherwise can we establish that the organization has in fact committed criminal acts unless we are able to prove whether individuals belonging to it have committed such crimes?

Does the trial, by the court, of individuals necessarily exclude the fact of the trial referring to the organization? In fact, what they are proposing is that the members of the organizations—S.S., Gestapo, and so on—have committed certain crimes in certain definite places, which crimes can be proved, and the whole group will be tried. It is immaterial whether the number of prisoners is 10 or 100 or any other number, but the fact that those individual prisoners are tried and convicted does, in fact, prove that the whole organization to which they belong is in effect a criminal organization. The way to establish that proof is not by the trial of the organization as such but by the trial of the individual members.

SIR DAVID MAXWELL FYFE. May we have a restatement of that, as it is of vital importance and we seem nearing an agreement?

GENERAL NIKITCHENKO. The Soviet Delegation consider that the Tribunal could try not merely individuals but groups. It would be immaterial whether those groups consist of members of the German Government, of the S.S., of the Gestapo, or any other organization, and it would also be immaterial how many of the persons accused were on trial at any one time, but the main point would be that the establishment of the criminal responsibility of those individuals would in effect establish the criminal responsibility of the whole organization to which they belong.

I would just like to note that the main difference between the Soviet and American plans appears to be that the American Delegation suggests the trial of the organization and then, having established the criminal character of the organization, to proceed from that to the trial of the individual adherents of the organization. The Soviet Delegation considers that that approach would not be the right one to secure conviction and punishment for individual members.

The second question is, what would be the consequences of a verdict by the court in regard to certain members of an organization upon other members of the same organization who might not be before the court? The Soviet criminal law is based on the fact of the individual criminal responsibility of the individual person. It is immaterial whether he committed some action alone or as a part of a gang; he has to carry individual responsibility for the action he has committed, one way or the other. We therefore consider that a decision of the court which establishes the criminal responsibility of the heads or the leaders of any organization of that kind automatically establishes the criminal responsibility of the various subordinate members of the organization. But that does not mean that the national courts or the occupation courts can apply punishment to all the members of an organization simply on the basis of the decision by the Tribunal of the trial of the individual members of that organization. . . .

MR. JUSTICE JACKSON. An essential step in declaring the criminal character of such organizations as we are dealing with here is not stated in our memorandum and perhaps caused this misunderstanding. We assumed it without stating it because in our philosophy it would be a necessary step. We propose to reach the organization through proof of what individuals did, just as you suggest. We take the same step of trying what the members did, what the common plan was through proof of what individuals agreed to, and we attribute what they did and agreed to do through the group to the organization. Then we take the next step of attributing the common principles that ran through the organization to the members. We, too, believe in individual responsibility and for that reason could not attribute the acts of the leaders to the members unless we proved that the acts of the leaders were within some common plan or conspiracy. The mere fact that leaders did some particular act, unless within the plan of the conspiracy and within its probable scope, might not bind others to that act. Therefore, we have to tie the acts of individuals to the organization and then the organizational purposes and methods to the individual members. But we do not think we are speaking of a great difference of substance. I think the difference is not as great as it appeared to be.

GENERAL NIKITCHENKO. I would just like to ask one question. Does the decision, when it has been reached in respect to an organization, by the court in this case, apply to all members of that organization; and, once the organization has been established as a criminal one, does that mean that punishment can be meted out to all members of that organization by national or other courts, or is it still necessary that those members should be put through a process of trial, either individually or in groups or gangs, or any other way?

MR. JUSTICE JACKSON. There would have to be an opportunity given to an individual, before he could be brought under the general plan, to show that there was a mistake in identification, that he was not a member in fact, or to show that he joined because he was forced to join, or some reason why the general finding of guilt should not be applied to him as an individual. He must have a chance to bring forward his individual situation, but he does not have a chance again to question the finding that the organization is guilty of particular plans or designs or offenses. That is settled in the one trial and all that he can thereafter be heard to say concerns his particular connection with the criminal design.

SIR DAVID MAXWELL FYFE. To put it quite bluntly, he could not be heard to say that the Gestapo, having been found to be a criminal organization in the trial, was not a criminal organization.

MR. JUSTICE JACKSON. Now let us see what we are trying to reach by this method that we might not reach otherwise. Let us suppose that there is a very active member of the S.S.—active in organizing, active in getting in new members—but he never took a personal part in a single crime. He helped to formulate the general plan; he knew about it; he knew the methods; he knew that their plan was to exterminate minorities, to run concentration camps, to do all these things; but you cannot prove by any witness that he was present when a single offense, standing by itself, was committed. By reason of his membership in this common criminal plan and by reason of his participation in it, we would expect to reach him. Now the difficulty is that there are several hundreds of thousands of members of these organizations. You cannot get witnesses, at least we haven't thought we could get witnesses, to prove where each was at all times and prove what he did. It is very hard to identify persons who are in uniform and to get accounts of their part in acts of the organized military or paramilitary units. Therefore, we would expect to be able to show what offenses were committed, and then every person who was a part of that general plan, whether he actually held the gun that shot the hostages or whether he sat at a desk somewhere and managed the accounting, would be responsible for the acts of the organization.

It may not bear on this particular plan directly, but it may bear on the thinking that is back of it as to whether one treats, in his system of jurisprudence, organizations as juridical persons, for purposes of trial. We in our system treat corporations and certain associations and organizations as juridical persons, and permit them to come into court and sue; and while we are not applying that principle in its entirety here, it perhaps makes it less unusual to us to think of trying an organization than it would if you do not treat organizations as juridical persons. I am wondering if your system does treat organizations under some circumstances as juridical persons.

PROFESSOR TRAININ. The question of juridical person is quite well known to the Soviet legal system, but it is applied in civil law, and they do not recognize this principle in their criminal law. In the criminal law it is necessary to bring home the responsibility to individual persons and not to condemn organizations. That does not in the least prevent the conviction of a person for adherence to or membership in a criminal organization, and the Soviet law provides for the trial of gangs or criminal associations, and it also provides for the trial of an individual for being a member of a criminal organization.

MR. JUSTICE JACKSON. I think the statement was made that the conviction of heads under the Soviet system would establish the responsibility of the members. That would be a somewhat more drastic application of the principle than we would be familiar with. It is not only necessary that the individual be responsible, which he is if he knowingly becomes a member of the gang, but that he have some opportunity in trial to defend what he has done. That is to say, you cannot, under our system, attribute guilt to a person who has not had an opportunity to appear and defend on the main issues. Therefore, it is necessary under our conception of reaching that individual that he shall have the right, at least by some representative arrangement, to be heard. That can be given him only, as we see it, if you put the organization on trial and give notice to the membership as far as can be given that the organization is on trial and that the members who are to be affected by the judgment may appear and defend it. That is, a mere decision that the heads of an organization had made a criminal conspiracy would not be sufficient to convict any member who was not a party to the trial or given an opportunity to be heard in some way, and that is why we have provided under the section on "Fair Trial for Defendants" [paragraph 14] that "reasonable notice shall be given to the defendants of the charges against them and of the opportunity to defend", that "such notice may be actual or constructive", and that "the Tribunal shall determine what constitutes reasonable notice . . . ."

Probably nobody, or at least few persons, in Germany would step forward and admit that they were members of these organizations. But under our system we would have to give them some notice and an opportunity to be heard. That does not necessarily mean that the Tribunal would have to hear each individual, but it would be necessary that in some way they have an opportunity to be heard before you can attribute guilt to them.

GENERAL NIKITCHENKO. Perhaps that point has not been quite clearly understood. According to the Soviet criminal law the members of a criminal organization are tried individually, but their being found guilty, if they are found guilty, does not mean that the organization to which they belong is declared to be a criminal organization. The Soviet law provides, in the case of criminal trials, for the trial of persons for infringement of the law itself and the commencement of the process of the courts against them. Whether it is a single individual or a gang, the man or the gang must be tried, and there is no automatic provision that because one has been convicted all other members are thereby pronounced guilty.

In fact, in the Soviet criminal law, when the trial of a member of an organization has proved that the organization to which he belongs is a criminal one, the responsibility is not on the individual to come forward and confess that he was a member of such an illegal organization. The responsibility is on the prosecuting organs of the court to bring a charge against that individual, and, when the prosecution brings such a charge and the individual is placed on trial, he is then given the opportunity of proving or disproving whether the accusations made against him by the prosecution are correct or whether he has acceptable legal defense against those accusations. . . .

JULY 24, 1945

GENERAL NIKITCHENKO. In article 7 of the charter I do not propose any change but would like to point out two considerations. Would it be proper really in speaking of major criminals to speak of them as carrying out some order of a superior? This is not a question of principle really, but I wonder if that is necessary when speaking of major criminals.

SIR DAVID MAXWELL FYFE. There are two points: first, they have already said they were just doing what Hitler said they should do; and secondly, in international law, certainly in some cases, superior orders were a defense, but in the sixth and seventh edition of Oppenheim it appears that they aren't a defense. If we don't make it clear, we may have some trouble on it.

GENERAL NIKITCHENKO. There is a misunderstanding. I wasn't against disallowing orders of a superior as a defense, but I thought that in regard to major criminals it would be improper to say that superior orders could be used in mitigation of punishment.

SIR DAVID MAXWELL FYFE. It seems to me difficult. Suppose someone said he was threatened to be shot if he did not carry out Hitler's orders. If he wasn't too important, the Tribunal might let him off with his life. It seems to be a matter for the Tribunal.

In one of the German cases on trial which were such a farce after the last war they did say that superior orders were no defense but could be taken into account on mitigation. That has been the general rule on superior orders in international law books.

GENERAL NIKITCHENKO. If the other heads of the delegations consider it best, we have no intention of pressing it. In general, it should be considered in mitigation; we think it is proper.

MR. JUSTICE JACKSON. Of course that was put in when we were considering trial of organizations, which would reach thousands of people who are not major criminals but would be reached through major criminals. And if you are going to get members of the Gestapo and S.S. through the conviction of the organization, it would be quite unfair if you would not take into consideration in fixing punishment the degree of real responsibility that they had. I think it would be a useful provision if we are to try organizations.

JUDGE FALCO. Leave it. Is it necessary to indicate to the Tribunal the reason for mitigation? If we say simply that orders are not a defense, it would seem to be left to the Tribunal to say that they may be a mitigation.

MR. JUSTICE JACKSON. That is about what we proposed originally —not an absolute defense but a mitigation.

SIR DAVID MAXWELL FYFE. The important part is that it should not be an absolute defense.

JUDGE FALCO. That is the important part. Must we add that that is the reason for the Tribunal to consider mitigation? . . .

CHARTER OF THE INTERNATIONAL MILITARY TRIBUNAL AT NUREMBERG

Constitution of the International Military Tribunal

Article 1 In pursuance of the agreement signed on the 8th August, 1945, by the Government of the United Kingdom of Great Britain and Northern Ireland, the Government of the United States of America, the Provisional Government of the French Republic and the Government of the Union of Soviet Socialist Republics, there shall be established an International Military Tribunal (hereinafter called "the Tribunal") for the just and prompt trial and punishment of the major war criminals of the European Axis.

Article 2 The Tribunal shall consist of four members, each with an alternate. One member and one alternate shall be appointed by each of the Signatories. The alternates shall, so far as they are able, be present at all sessions of the Tribunal. In case of illness of any member of the Tribunal or his incapacity for some other reason to fulfil his functions, his alternate shall take his place.

Article 3 Neither the Tribunal, its members nor their alternates can be challenged by the Prosecution, or by the Defendants or their Counsel. Each Signatory may replace its member of the Tribunal or his alternate for reasons of health or for other good reasons, except that no replacement may take place during a Trial, other than by an alternate.

Article 4 (a) The presence of all four members of the Tribunal or the alternate for any absent member shall be necessary to constitute the quorum.

(b) The members of the Tribunal shall, before any trial begins, agree among themselves upon the selection from their number of a President, and the President shall hold office during that trial, or as may otherwise be agreed by a vote of not less than three members. The principle of rotation of presidency for successive trials is agreed. If, however, a session of the Tribunal takes place on the territory of one of the four Signatories, the representative of the Signatory on the Tribunal shall preside.

(c) Save as aforesaid the Tribunal shall take decisions by a majority vote and in case the votes are evenly divided, the vote of the President shall be decisive: provided always that convictions and sentences shall only be imposed by affirmative votes of at least three members of the Tribunal.

Article 5 In case of need and depending on the number of the matters to be tried, other Tribunals may be set up; and the establishment, functions, and procedure of each Tribunal shall be identical, and shall be governed by this Charter.

JURISDICTION AND GENERAL PRINCIPLES

Article 6 The Tribunal established by the Agreement referred to in Article 1 hereof for the trial and punishment of the major war criminals of the European Axis countries shall have the power to try and punish persons who, acting in the interests of the European Axis countries, whether as individuals or as members of organisations, committed any of the following crimes.

The following acts, or any of them, are crimes coming within the jurisdiction of the Tribunal for which there shall be individual responsibility:

(a) Crimes against peace: namely, planning, preparation, initiation or waging of a war of aggression, or a war in violation of international treaties, agreements or assurances, or participation in a common plan or conspiracy for the accomplishment of any of the foregoing.

(b) War crimes: namely, violations of the laws or customs of war. Such violations shall include, but not be limited to, murder, ill-treatment or deportation to slave labour or for any other purpose of civilian population of or in occupied territory, murder or ill-treatment of prisoners of war or persons on the seas, killing of hostages, plunder of public property, wanton destruction of cities, towns or villages, or devastation not justified by military necessity.

(c) Crimes against humanity: namely, murder, extermination, enslavement, deportation, and other inhumane acts committed against any civilian population, before or during the war, or persecutions on political, racial or religious grounds in execution of or in connection with any crime within the jurisdiction of the Tribunal, whether or not in violation of the domestic law of the country where perpetrated.

Leaders, organisers, instigators, and accomplices participating in the formulation or execution of a common plan or conspiracy to commit any of the foregoing crimes are responsible for all acts performed by any persons in execution of such plan.

Article 7 The official position of Defendants, whether as Heads of State or responsible officials in Government Departments, shall not be considered as freeing them from responsibility or mitigating punishment.

Article 8 The fact that the Defendant acted pursuant to order of his Government or of a superior shall not free him from responsibility, but may be considered in mitigation of punishment if the Tribunal determines that justice so requires.

Article 9 At the trial of any individual member of any group or organisation the Tribunal may declare (in connection with any act of which the individual may be convicted) that the group or organisation of which the individual was a member was a criminal organisation.

After receipt of the Indictment the Tribunal shall give such notice as it thinks fit that the Prosecution intends to ask the Tribunal to make such declaration and any member of the organisation will be entitled to apply to the Tribunal for leave to be heard by the Tribunal upon the question of the criminal character of the organisation. The Tribunal shall have power to allow or reject the application. If the application is allowed, the Tribunal may direct in what manner the applicants shall be represented and heard.

Article 10 In cases where a group or organisation is declared criminal by the Tribunal, the competent national authority of any

Signatory shall have the right to bring individuals to trial for membership therein before national, military or occupation courts. In any such case the criminal nature of the group or organisation is considered proved and shall not be questioned.

Article 11 Any person convicted by the Tribunal may be charged before a national, military or occupation court, referred to in Article 10 of this Charter, with a crime other than of membership in a criminal group or organisation, and such court may, after convicting him, impose upon him punishment independent of and additional to the punishment imposed by the Tribunal for participation in the criminal activities of such group or organisation.

Article 12 The Tribunal shall have the right to take proceedings against a person charged with crimes set out in Article 6 of this Charter in his absence, if he has not been found or if the Tribunal, for any reason, finds it necessary, in the interests of justice, to conduct the hearing in his absence.

Article 13 The Tribunal shall draw up rules for its procedure. These rules shall not be inconsistent with the provisions of this Charter.

COMMITTEE FOR THE INVESTIGATION AND PROSECUTION OF MAJOR WAR CRIMINALS

Article 14 Each Signatory shall appoint a Chief Prosecutor for the investigation of the charges against, and the prosecution of, major war criminals.

The Chief Prosecutor shall act as a committee for the following purposes:

(a) to agree upon a plan of the individual work of each of the Chief Prosecutors and his staff;

(b) to settle the final designation of major war criminals to be tried by the Tribunal;

(c) to approve the Indictment and the documents to be submitted therewith;

(d) to lodge the Indictment and the accompanying documents with the Tribunal;

(e) to draw up and recommend to the Tribunal for its approval draft rules of procedure, contemplated by Article 13 of this Charter. The Tribunal shall have power to accept, with or without amendments, or to reject, the rules so recommended.

The Committee shall act in all the above matters by a majority vote and shall appoint a Chairman as may be convenient and in accordance with the principle of rotation: provided that if there is an equal division of vote concerning the designation of a Defendant to be tried by the Tribunal, or the crimes with which he shall be charged, that proposal will be adopted which was made by the party which proposed that the particular Defendant be tried, or the particular charge be preferred against him.

Article 15 The Chief Prosecutors shall individually, and acting in collaboration with one another, also undertake the following duties:

(a) investigation, collection, and production before or at the Trial of all necessary evidence;

(b) the preparation of the Indictment for approval by the Committee in accordance with paragraph (c) of Article 14 hereof;

(c) the preliminary examination of all necessary witnesses and of the Defendants;

(d) to act as prosecutor at the Trial;

(e) to appoint representatives to carry out such duties as may be assigned to them;

(f) to undertake such other matters as may appear necessary to them for the purposes of the preparation for and conduct of the Trial.

It is understood that no witness or Defendant detained by any Signatory shall be taken out of the possession of that Signatory without its assent.

FAIR TRIAL FOR DEFENDANTS

Article 16 In order to ensure fair trial for the Defendants, the following procedure shall be followed:

(a) The Indictment shall include full particulars specifying in detail the charges against the Defendants. A copy of the Indictment and of all the documents lodged with the Indictment, translated into a language which he understands, shall be furnished to the Defendant at a reasonable time before the Trial.

(b) During any preliminary examination or trial of a Defendant he shall have the right to give any explanation relevant to the charges made against him.

(c) A preliminary examination of a Defendant and his Trial should be conducted in, or translated into, a language which the Defendant understands.

(d) A Defendant shall have the right to conduct his own defence before the Tribunal or to have the assistance of Counsel.

(e) A Defendant shall have the right through himself or through his Counsel to present evidence at the Trial in support of his defence, and to cross-examine any witness called by the Prosecution.

POWERS OF THE TRIBUNAL AND CONDUCT OF THE TRIAL

Article 17 The Tribunal shall have the power:

(a) to summon witnesses to the Trial and to require their attendance and testimony and to put questions to them;

(b) to interrogate any Defendant;

(c) to require the production of documents and other evidentiary material;

(d) to administer oaths to witnesses;

(e) to appoint officers for the carrying out of any task designated by the Tribunal including the power to have evidence taken on commission.

Article 18 The Tribunal shall:

(a) confine the Trial strictly to an expeditious hearing of the issues raised by the charges;

(b) take strict measures to prevent any action which will cause unreasonable delay, and rule out irrelevant issues and statements of any kind whatsoever;

(c) deal summarily with any contumacy, imposing appropriate punishment, including exclusion of any Defendant or his Counsel from some or all further proceedings, but without prejudice to the determination of the charges.

Article 19 The Tribunal shall not be bound by technical rules of evidence. It shall adopt and apply to the greatest possible extent expeditious and non-technical procedure, and shall admit any evidence which it deems to have probative value.

Article 20 The Tribunal may require to be informed of the nature of any evidence before it is offered so that it may rule upon the relevance thereof.

Article 21 The Tribunal shall not require proof of facts of common knowledge but shall take judicial notice thereof. It shall also take judicial notice of official governmental documents and reports of the United Nations, including the acts and documents of the committees set up in the various Allied countries for the investigation of war crimes, and the records and findings of military or other Tribunals of any of the United Nations.

Article 22 The permanent seat of the Tribunal shall be in Berlin. The first meetings of the members of the Tribunal and of the Chief Prosecutors shall be held at Berlin in a place to be designated by the Control Council for Germany. The first trial shall be held at Nuremberg, and any subsequent trials shall be held at such places as the Tribunal may decide.

Article 23 One or more of the Chief Prosecutors may take part in the prosecution at each Trial. The function of any Chief Prosecutor may be discharged by him personally, or by any person or persons authorised by him.

The function of Counsel for a Defendant may be discharged at the Defendant's request by any Counsel professionally qualified to conduct cases before the courts of his own country, or by any other person who may be specially authorised thereto by the Tribunal.

Article 24 The proceedings at the trial shall take the following course:

(a) The Indictment shall be read in court.

(b) The Tribunal shall ask each Defendant whether he pleads "guilty" or "not guilty."

(c) The Prosecution shall make an opening statement.

(d) The Tribunal shall ask the Prosecution and the Defence

what evidence (if any) they wish to submit to the Tribunal, and the Tribunal shall rule upon admissibility of any such evidence.

(e) The witnesses for the Prosecution shall be examined and after the witnesses for the Defence. Thereafter such rebutting evidence as may be held by the Tribunal to be admissible shall be called by either the Prosecution or the Defence.

(f) The Tribunal may put any question to any witness and to any Defendant, at any time.

(g) The Prosecution and the Defence shall interrogate and may cross-examine any witnesses and any Defendant who gives testimony.

(h) The Defence shall address the court.

(i) The Prosecution shall address the court.

(j) Each Defendant may make a statement to the Tribunal.

(k) The Tribunal shall deliver judgment and pronounce sentence.

Article 25 All official documents shall be produced, and all court proceedings conducted, in English, French, and Russian, and in the language of the Defendant. So much of the record and of the proceedings may also be translated into the language of any country in which the Tribunal is sitting, as the Tribunal considers desirable in the interests of justice and public opinion.

JUDGMENT AND SENTENCE

Article 26 The Judgment of the Tribunal as to the guilt or the innocence of any Defendant shall give the reasons on which it is based, and shall be final and not subject to review.

Article 27 The Tribunal shall have the right to impose upon a Defendant, on conviction, death or such other punishment as shall be determined by it to be just.

Article 28 In addition to any punishment imposed by it, the Tribunal shall have the right to deprive the convicted person of any stolen property and order its delivery to the Control Council for Germany.

Article 29 In case of guilt, sentences shall be carried out in accordance with the orders of the Control Council for Germany, which may at any time reduce or otherwise alter the sentences, but may not increase the severity thereof. If the Control Council for Germany, after any Defendant has been convicted and sentenced, discovers fresh evidence which, in its opinion, would found a fresh charge against him, the Council shall report accordingly to the Committee established under Article 14 hereof for such action as they may consider proper, having regard to the interests of justice.

EXPENSES

Article 30 The expenses of the Tribunal and of the Trials shall be charged by the Signatories against the funds allotted for maintenance of the Control Council for Germany.

NURÉMBERG TRIALS
THE JODL DEFENCE*

July 19, 1946
as presented by his attorney Dr. Exner

In general, one can only be made responsible for what one does criminally when one should not do it, and for what one has criminally neglected to do when one ought to have done it. What an officer or an official has or has not got to do is a question of competence. So this is where the problem of competence assumes its importance for us. Let us look at it more closely:

Jodl is accused of having planned and prepared certain wars which were breaches of international law. This reproach would be justified only if it was within his competence to examine, before he carried out his task, the legality of the war which might be waged, and to make his co-operation dependent on this decision. This must be very definitely contested. Whether or not to wage a war is a political question and is the politician's concern. The question of how to wage war is the only question concerning the Armed Forces. The Armed Forces can suggest that the war is, in view of the opponent's strength, too risky, or that the war cannot be waged at a particular season, but the final decision rests with the politicians.

I could, to be sure, imagine that the Chief of the Armed Forces Operations Staff might become at least morally guilty of complicity in a war of aggression if he had incited the decisive quarters to bring about a war, or if, drawing attention to military

* From the official text in the English language, Proceedings 19 July 1946–29 July 1946, excerpts from pages 20–37.

superiority, he had advised the political leadership to exploit the propitious moment in order to carry out extensive plans of conquest. In such a case one could call him an accomplice, because he, over and above his military task, intervened in politics and provoked the decision for war. But if he plans and carries out the plan of a possible war, that is, in case the political leadership decides on war, he does nothing but his evident duty.

One should consider the extraordinary consequences which would arise from a different conception: The competent authority would declare war, and the Chief of the General Staff, who regards this war as contrary to international law, would fail to co-operate. Or the Chief of General Staff happens to be of the same opinion as the head of the State, but one of the army commanders has objections and refuses to march, while another one has doubts and has to think it over first. Can war be waged at all in this case, be it a war of defense or a war of aggression? . . .

The truth is this: As long as there is no superstate authority which impartially establishes whether, in a concrete case, such a duty does exist for the individual, and as long as there is no superstate authority which will protect against punishment for high treason and desertion people who fulfill this duty, an officer cannot be held criminally for a breach of the peace. Whatever the circumstances, one thing must be pointed out: On the one hand the Prosecution reproaches the generals for not having been simply soldiers, but also politicians; on the other hand, it demands of them that they should remonstrate against the political leadership and sabotage its resolutions—in short, that they should not simply be soldiers, but politicians . . .

It is true that without his generals Hitler could not have waged the wars. But only a layman can construct a responsibility on that basis. If the generals do not do their job, there is no war. But one must add: if the infantryman does not march, if his rifle does not fire, if he has nothing to clothe himself with and nothing to eat, there is no war. Is therefore the soldier, the gunsmith, the shoemaker, the farmer guilty of complicity in the war? The argument is based on a confusion between guilt and causation. All these persons, and many others too, effectively co-operated in the waging of the war. But can one therefore attribute any guilt to them? Does Henry Ford share in the responsibility for the thousands of accidents which his cars cause every year? If an affirmative answer is given to the question of causation, the question of guilt is still not answered . . .

Let us assume that Jodl was sure that the war was illegal and that he had, for reasons of conscience, refused to collaborate. What difference would there then have been between him and a soldier who throws away his rifle in battle and retreats? Both of them would be liable to the death penalty for disobeying orders in war.

I know that the United States is generous enough to respect a soldier who, for religious reasons, refuses to take up arms, and not treat them as we do. But that applies only to religious scruples, and doubtless does not apply to a man who, owing to objections based on international law, does not co-operate in the war decided on by the political leadership. One would object that it is not his affair, not an affair of his conscience to examine the admissibility of the war, but that this is the duty of the responsible state authorities. According to continental law, one would not even stop to consider such an excuse for refusing obedience. . . .

May it please the Tribunal, there is an old saying in criminal law, a saying which I always find cited in foreign decisions too, that *actus non facit reum nisi mens sit rea.* Two things go to make a crime; the *actus,* the objective side of the crime, the deed, and the *mens rea,* the subjective side or guilt. The Prosecution is involved in an odd contradiction there; in some cases they stress the *mens rea* and fail to see that the criminal *actus* is lacking: I have shown this in the case of the above-mentioned marginal comments, which do not represent any illegal actions, but at most could allow one to infer an illegal frame of mind. In other cases the Prosecution look only at the *actus,* but does not ask whether a *mens rea* is also present. This second mistake is more dangerous, as here the outside of the crime is visible to everyone and it is often only a delicate psychological examination that can lead to the conclusion that there is no *mens rea* which corresponds to the *actus.* We will come to speak of this further on.

With regard to the action, what is meant is behavior declared criminal by the Charter. This behavior can consist of positive action or of omission. If a father sees his child drowning while bathing and does nothing to save him although he could have done so, we declare him guilty either of murder or of killing by negligence, according to the degree of his guilt. This commission of a crime by omission is important in this Trial too, for the Prosecution repeatedly stress that Jodl was present at this or that meeting, at this or that speech. On one single page of the Anglo-American trial brief the phrase "Jodl was present at . . ." occurs six times. What does this mean legally? Being present at and listening to things can be of great importance with regard to the evaluation of a later deed, for the doer cannot excuse himself by saying "I didn't know" if he participated in the discussion of a plan. But mere presence does not in itself make one an accomplice. According to British law, even actual presence when a crime is committed makes one an accomplice only if encouragement is added. The same applies in German law. But where this is not involved, to lay stress on a person's presence when a criminal intention was discussed can only amount to a reproach that "he knew about and tolerated it."

Today we often hear this reproach of having tolerated crimes. Not only in this court. The whole German people are reproached for having tolerated a criminal regime and the annihilation of millions of Jews. Undoubtedly a crime can also be committed by tolerating things. But to make it a serious criminal charge, that is, one of intentional killing, two prerequisites must be fulfilled: 1) The subjective side: The perpetrator must have known that the victim would meet his death if he did not intervene; 2) he must have been in duty bound and able to prevent this death . . .

GENEVA CONVENTION RELATIVE TO THE PROTECTION OF CIVILIAN PERSONS IN TIME OF WAR*

August 12, 1949

The undersigned Plenipotentiaries of the Governments represented at the Diplomatic Conference held at Geneva from April 21 to August 12, 1949, for the purpose of establishing a Convention for the Protection of Civilian Persons in Time of War, have agreed as follows:

PART I: GENERAL PROVISIONS

Article 1 The High Contracting Parties undertake to respect and to ensure respect for the present Convention in all circumstances.

Article 2 In addition to the provisions which shall be implemented in peacetime, the present Convention shall apply to all cases of declared war or of any other armed conflict which may arise between two or more of the High Contracting Parties, even if the state of war is not recognized by one of them.

The Convention shall also apply to all cases of partial or total occupation of the territory of a High Contracting Party, even if the said occupation meets with no armed resistance.

Although one of the Powers in conflict may not be a party to the present Convention, the Powers who are parties thereto shall remain bound by it in their mutual relations. They shall furthermore be bound by the Convention in relation to the said Power, if the latter accepts and applies the provisions thereof.

* English language text from a copy certified by the Swiss Federal Council.

Article 3 In the case of armed conflict not of an international character occurring in the territory of one of the High Contracting Parties, each Party to the conflict shall be bound to apply, as a minimum, the following provisions:

(1) Persons taking no active part in the hostilities, including members of armed forces who have laid down their arms and those placed *hors de combat* by sickness, wounds, detention, or any other cause, shall in all circumstances be treated humanely, without any adverse distinction founded on race, colour, religion or faith, sex, birth or wealth, or any other similar criteria.

To this end, the following acts are and shall remain prohibited at any time and in any place whatsoever with respect to the above-mentioned persons:

(a) violence to life and person, in particular murder of all kinds, mutilation, cruel treatment and torture;

(b) taking of hostages;

(c) outrages upon personal dignity, in particular humiliating and degrading treatment;

(d) the passing of sentences and the carrying out of executions without previous judgment pronounced by a regularly constituted court, affording all the judicial guarantees which are recognized as indispensable by civilized peoples.

(2) The wounded and sick shall be collected and cared for.

An impartial humanitarian body, such as the International Committee of the Red Cross, may offer its services to the Parties to the conflict.

The Parties to the conflict should further endeavour to bring into force, by means of special arrangements, all or part of the other provisions of the present Convention.

The application of the preceding provisions shall not affect the legal status of the Parties to the conflict.

THE UNITED STATES ARMY FIELD MANUAL

The Law of Land Warfare, 1956

501. Responsibility for Acts of Subordinates

In some cases, military commanders may be responsible for war crimes committed by subordinate members of the armed forces, or other persons subject to their control. Thus, for instance, when troops commit massacres and atrocities against the civilian population of occupied territory or against prisoners of war, the responsibility may rest not only with the actual perpetrators but also with the command. Such a responsibility arises directly when the acts in questions have been committed in pursuance of an order of the commander concerned. The commander is also responsible if he has actual knowledge, or should have knowledge, through reports received by him or through other means, that troops or other persons subject to his control are about to commit or have committed a war crime and he fails to take the necessary and reasonable steps to insure compliance with the law of war or to punish violators thereof. . . .

505. Universality of Jurisdiction

. . . b. *Persons Charged with War Crimes.* The United States normally punishes war crimes as such only if they are committed by enemy nationals or by persons serving the interests of the enemy State. Violations of the law of war committed by persons subject to military law of the United States will usually constitute violations of the Uniform Code of Military Justice and, if so, will be prosecuted under that Code. . . . Commanding officers of United States troops must insure that war crimes committed by members of their forces against enemy personnel are promptly and adequately punished.

509. DEFENSE OF SUPERIOR ORDERS

a. The fact that the law of war has been violated pursuant to an order of a superior authority, whether military or civil, does not deprive the act in question of its character as a war crime, nor does it constitute a defense in the trial of an accused individual, unless he did not know and could not reasonably have been expected to know that the act was unlawful. In all cases where the order is held not to constitute a defense to an allegation of war crime, the fact that the individual was acting pursuant to orders may be considered in mitigation of punishment.

b. In considering the question of whether a superior order constitutes a valid defense, the court shall take into consideration the fact that obedience to lawful military orders is the duty of every member of the armed forces; that the latter cannot be expected, in conditions of war discipline, to weigh scrupulously the legal merits of the order received; that certain rules of warfare may be controversial; or that an act otherwise amounting to a war crime may be done in obedience to orders conceived as a measure of reprisal. At the same time it must be borne in mind that members of the armed forces are bound to obey only lawful orders.

510. GOVERNMENT OFFICIALS

The fact that a person who committed an act which constitutes a war crime acted as the head of a State or as a responsible government official does not relieve him from responsibility for his act.

BIBLIOGRAPHY

ON MY LAI

Magazines

Life. Dec. 5, 1969, p. 36
March 5, 1971, p. 22

National Review. Oct. 22, 1971, pp. 1172-3

Newsweek. March 1, 1971, pp. 21-2
April 12, 1971, pp. 27-34

New York Times. Feb. 24, 1971, p. 20
Feb. 25, 1971, p. 24

New Yorker. Jan. 22, 1972, p. 34
Jan. 29, 1972, p. 40

Time. March 8, 1971, p. 18
April 12, 1971, pp. 13-21

Books

Lieutenant Calley: His Own Story as told to John Sack, Viking Press, 1971.

A. Everett, K. Johnson, H. Rosenthal. *Calley.* Dell Publishing, 1971.

R. Hammer. *The Court Martial of Lt. Calley.* Coward, McCann & Geoghegan, 1971.

S. M. Hersh. *My Lai 4, A Report on the Massacre and its Aftermath.* New York: Vintage, 1970.

Opton and Duckles. *My Lai: It Never Happened and Besides, They Deserved It.* Berkeley: Wright Institute, 1970.

T. Taylor. *Nuremberg and Vietnam.* New York: Quadrangle Books, 1970.

T. Tiede. *Calley: Soldier or Killer?* Pinnacle Books, 1971.

ON COLLECTIVE RESPONSIBILITY AND RELATED TOPICS

K. Baier. "Moral Obligation," *American Philosophical Quarterly,* Vol. 3, No. 3, July, 1966, p. 210.

S. Bates. "Responsibility of 'Random Collections,'" *Ethics,* Vol. 81, 1971, p. 343.

M. Brand. *The Nature of Human Action.* Glenview: Scott Foresman, 1970.

R. Brandt. "Blameworthiness and Obligations," *Essays in Moral Philosophy,* ed. A. I. Meldon, Seattle: University of Washington Press, 1958, pp. 82-107.

M. Brodbeck. "Methodological Individualism: Definition and Reduction," *Philosophy of Science,* Vol. 25, 1958, pp. 1-22.

P. Calvocoressi. *Nuremberg: The Facts, the Law and the Consequences.* New York: Macmillan, 1948.

D. E. Cooper. "Collective Responsibility," *Philosophy,* July, 1968, Vol. XLIII, No. 165, p. 258.

———. "Collective Responsibility—Again," *Philosophy,* April, 1969, Vol. XLIV, No. 168, p. 153.

N. Cousins. "The Non-Obliterators," *Saturday Review,* April 8, 1944, p. 14.

R. S. Downie. "Collective Responsibility," *Philosophy,* Jan., 1969, Vol. XLIV, No. 167, p. 66.

———. *Government and Morality.* London: Macmillan, 1964.

———. *Roles and Values.* London: Methuen, 1971; U. S. A.: Barnes and Noble.

———. "Social Roles and Moral Responsibility," *Philosophy,* Jan., 1964.

J. Feinberg. "Collective Responsibility," *Journal of Philosophy,* Vol. LXV, No. 7, 1968.

J. C. Ford. "The Morality of Obliteration Bombing," *Theological Studies,* Vol. 5, 1944, p. 261.

D. P. Gauthier. *Practical Reasoning.* Oxford: Clarenden Press, 1963.

H. Gomperz. "Individual, Collective, and Social Responsibility," *Ethics,* LXIX, April, 1939.

H. L. A. Hart. "The Ascription of Responsibility and Rights," *Proceedings of the Aristotelian Society,* 1948-49, Section III.

———. *The Concept of Law.* Oxford: Clarendon Press, 1961.

———. "Legal and Moral Obligation," *Essays in Moral Philosophy,* ed. A. I. Meldon, Seattle: U. of Washington Press, 1958.

V. Held. "Can a Random Collection of Individuals be Morally Responsible?" *Journal of Philosophy,* Vol. LXVII, No. 14, July 23, 1970, p. 461.

H. Kelsen. "Collective and Individual Responsibility in International Law with Particular Regard to the Punishment of War Criminals," 31 *Calif. Law Review,* 1953, p. 531.

L. Kenner. "On Blaming," *Mind,* April, 1969, Col. LXXVL, No. 302, p. 238.

H. D. Lewis. "Collective Responsibility," *Philosophy,* Vol. XXIII, No. 84, Jan. 1948, p. 3.

G. Lewy. "Superior Orders, Nuclear Warfare, and the Dictates of Conscience," *The American Political Science Review,* Vol. 55, 1961, p. 3.

D. MacDonald. *Memoirs of a Revolutionist.* New York: Farrar, Straus and Cudahy, 1957, pp. 33-72.

H. Morris. (ed.) *Guilt and Shame.* California: Wadsworth, 1971.

K. Popper. *The Open Society and Its Enemies.* London: Routledge & Kegan Paul, 1945.

C. Strang. "What if Everyone Did That?" *The Durham University Journal,* Vol. LIII, No. 1, Dec. 1960, p. 5.

W. H. Walsh. "Pride, Shame, and Responsibility," *The Philosophical Quarterly,* Vol. 20, No. 78, Jan. 1970, pp. 1-13.

M. Walzer. "Moral Judgment in War," *Dissent,* Vol. 14, No. 3, 1967, p. 284.

R. Wasserstrom. "The Laws of War," *The Monist,* 56, Jan. 1972.

———. "The Relevance of Nuremberg," *Philosophy and Public Affairs,* I (Fall, 1971)

J. W. N. Watkins. "Historical Explanation in the Social Sciences," *British Journal for the Philosophy of Science,* Vol. 8, 1957, p. 104.

A. White. "On Being Obliged to Act," Royal Institute of Philosophy Lectures, *The Human Agent,* Vol. I, 1966-67. St. Martin's Press, p. 64.

R. K. Woetzel. *The Nuremberg Trials in International Law.* London: Stevens & Sons Ltd., 1962, Chapter 5, "The Criminal Responsibility of the Individual under International Law," p. 26.

2 3 4 5 6 7 8 9 10 11 12 13 14 15-B-78 77 76 75 74